Let's Learn Korean Alphabet 한글
with King Sejong the Great

Let's Learn Korean Alphabet 한글

with King Sejong the Great

Yu Eunsil

Hangeul, characters for all the sounds of nature

Koreans speak the Korean language (Hangungmal **한국말** or Hangugeo **한국어**) and write using Korean characters, Hangeul (**한글**). Chinese characters have been widely used in Asia for a long time, just like the Roman alphabet was once used commonly in Europe, regardless of race or nationality. Thus, our Korean ancestors used Chinese characters until the invention of Hangeul.

One can write with the same characters when two languages are similar. However, writing Korean speech using Chinese characters is difficult because the Korean language is completely different from the Chinese language. The ancient Koreans, mainly of aristocratic class, put much effort into learning Chinese characters to express themselves. Meanwhile, it was nearly impossible for ordinary people to learn to read or write Chinese characters, which put them at a disadvantage in many ways. The recognition of such problems led to the creation of Hangeul.

In the prehistoric age, early humans exchanged and recorded information using primitive methods, such as making knots with rope or painting murals on cave walls or rocks. Such murals gradually became pictorial symbols and finally turned into pictographs and hieroglyphics. The Roman alphabet is a set of letters originally based on pictographs that represent sounds. The historical shape of the letter 'O' was ' ', resembling the shape of the eye, while the shape of 'P' used to be ' ', showing the shape of the mouth. After being adopted in Egypt, these pictographs passed through Sinai, Sem, Phoenicia, and Greece, undergoing changes over time and differing cultures to finally become the Roman alphabet. In the Roman alphabet, the letter 'A' used to be 'alphe', meaning 'ox', but its original meaning was later lost and only the letter 'A', which stands for the first sound of the word (alphe) remained.

Even after the Chinese character system had developed to be much more complex and scientific, its tens of thousands of pictographic letters are still ideographs, each expressing its unique meaning. The Japanese people have used Chinese characters throughout history. Around the 9th century, however, the Japanese developed 'Kana', a new set of letters used along with Chinese characters. However, Korean characters were neither pictographs nor ideographs, but a simple and reasoned alphabet to represent the sounds of the Korean language.

The creation of Hangeul

Hangeul is nearly the only alphabet invented for a distinct purpose, with its principles published in an official document. Hangeul was created by King Sejong the Great (1397-1450) of the Joseon Dynasty on December 1443, the 25th year of his reign. At that time, King Sejong named his creation 'Hun (enlightening) - Min (people) - Jeong (correct) – Eum (sound)'. «Sejong Chronicles» records these facts in detail.

After creating Hunminjeongeum himself, King Sejong ordered the scholars of Jiphyeonjeon(National Academic Institute of the Joseon Dynasty) to write a thorough explanation of the basic principles and instructions for writing Hangeul for the people to learn. Following the King's order, the scholars published a book in early September 1446, which was three years after the creation of Hangeul, naming it 《Hunminjeongeum》. Unfortunately the existence of 《Hunminjeongeum》 was known only through records. It was not until 1940 that the physical book was discovered, finally coming out of the darkness for the first time nearly 500 years later. Art collector Jun Hyungpil purchased the historical document which was discovered at a private house in Andong, Gyeongsangbuk-do. Ownership then passed to Gansong Museum in Seoul. 《Hunminjeongeum》 was listed as the National Treasure of Korea No. 70 in 1962 and was listed in UNESCO's Memory of the World Register in 1997. It is unique in world history that a book was published to explain the purpose, the principles, and the instructions of a newly created character.

King Sejong the Great's Statue in Gwanghwamun Plaza

The purpose of the invention of Hunminjeongeum

King Sejong himself describes the purpose of the invention of Hunminjeongeum in Uhae Suhmoon (King's preface) of 《Hunminjeongeum》 as follows:

"We have not had our own letters until now, so we use Chinese characters. However, these characters cannot fully express our spoken language becaue it is completely different from that of China. Some of my people cannot properly express what they think in writing. I feel sorry for this, so I have created 28 new letters called Hunminjeongeum. My people shall be able to learn them quickly and to use them daily."

As we can see from the excerpt above, King Sejong's philosophy for Hunminjeongeum included independence from Chinese characters, pragmatic lines of thoughts, and democratic ideas for all people.

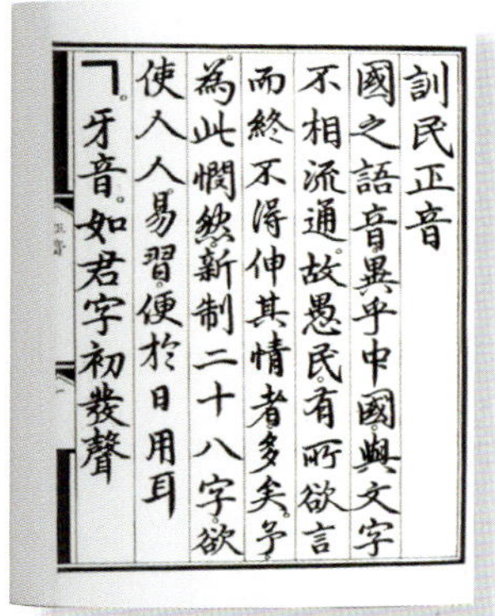 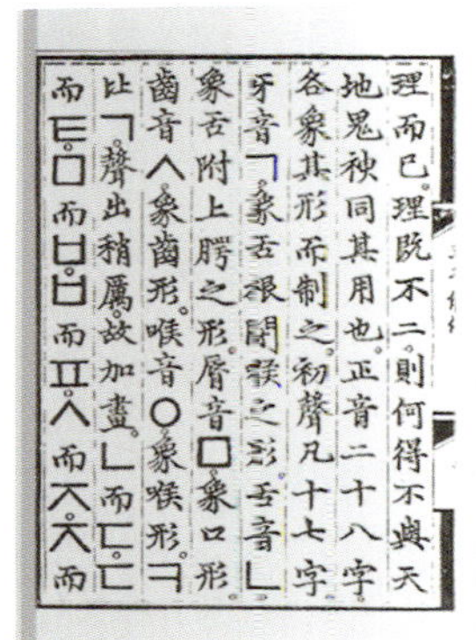 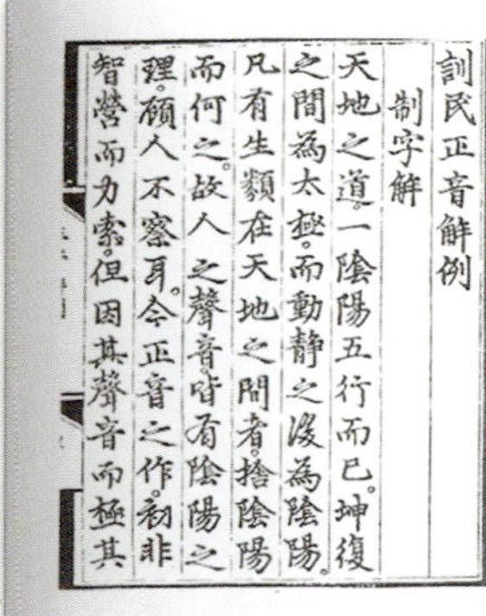

Left: 《Hunminjeongeum》Uhjae Suhmoon(king's preface)
Right: 《Hunminjeongeum》Jejahae(explanation or the principle of creation of letters)

The fundamental principles of Hunminjeongeum

The fundamental principles of Hunminjeongeum are **Yin-Yang** and **the Five Elements**, which are well expressed in 《Hunminjeongeum》 as follows:

> *"The fundamental principles that govern the universe are Yin-Yang and the Five Elements. They exist in the speech of humankind, but the ancient people failed to recognize them. We now deeply pursue the principles that are involved in human speech."*
>
> *"Since there is a sound in the universe, there should be a corresponding character."*
>
> *"All things in the universe have their own shapes and sounds, thus the only fundamental principles apply to them."*

Now let us grasp the meaning of the three quotes above. All things in the universe have their own shapes and sounds, so humankind living in the universe has its own sound.

Humans invent characters to express speech, so characters should follow the principles of the universe. When King Sejong created Hangeul, people thought that the principles of the universe were Yin-Yang and the Five Elements. Therefore, Yin-Yang and the Five Elements were the basis for the creation of Hangeul.

Yin-Yang and the Five Elements have been the framework for explaining all the phenomena of life and the universe in Eastern Asia since ancient times. It was a way of thinking, an explanation of the mechanisms and logistics of everything in the universe rather than a philosophy or concept. People in ancient times were unaware that the earth rotates on its axis and revolves around the sun regularly. However, they recognized the principles of life and the universe by observing the change of day into night (Yin-Yang) and the change of the seasons (the Five Elements). Modern science regards the earth's rotation and revolution as having the greatest influences on our lives.

Because the earth rotates on its axis, we have day and night. The property of natural phenomena during the day are called Yang, while that during the night are called Yin. Opposing phenomena such as the opening (Yang) and closing (Yin) of the mouth and breathing in (Yin) and out (Yang) are understood based on the principle. Human beings, their lives, and their speech are all included in these natural phenomena.

The earth revolving around the sun generates the seasons with their different properties. Each year consists of spring, summer, fall, and winter, as well as late summer which is considered a critical time when Yang turns into Yin between summer and fall. Spring and summer is Yang, and fall and winter is Yin. Now let us briefly review the characteristics of each season.

Spring is the season when new lives are born. Animals in hibernation wake up, and sprouts emerge from the frozen ground, penetrating the soil and stones. Young grasses, green leaves, and rejuvenated trees signal the arrival of spring. Spring brings newborn lives, and its symbol is a tree.

Yin-Yang

Rotation of the earth on its axis

Yang

day, bright, sun

hot, warm

man, open

breathe out

expand

bloom

stand up

Yin

night, dark, moon

cold, chill

woman, close

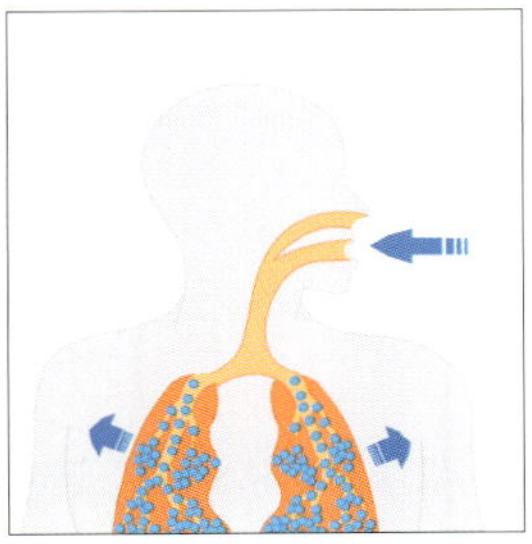

breathe in

contract

pucker

lie down

Summer is the season for the vigorous growth of life. Trees and their leaves become abundant, and bugs are active, flying in the hot air. It all feels like the flames rising up from firewood. Summer brings growth, and its symbol is fire.

Late summer is the season when the hot weather starts to cool down. The growth which once seemed endless ceases, and then active changes begin in the soil. Numerous minute lives bring about changes. Late summer brings changes, and its symbol is soil.

Fall is the season that brings life's activity to fruition. Grains and fruits ripen with their completed shapes and colors. People harvest the results of their efforts in the golden fields. Trees take back the energy from their leaves, making themselves stout for winter. Trees' annual rings become hardened in the fall. Fall brings the harvest, and its symbol is metal.

Winter is the season for the preservation of life. Trees drop their leaves and store energy within their branches and twigs in preparation for the cold weather. People also reduce their activities and quietly prepare for a new year. Although the length of nighttime shortens after the winter solstice, spring is still far away. The life inside of firm seeds quietly waits for the coming spring. White snow heaped up on the ground covers the preserved lives. All living things are born from water, and the most important factor for life preservation is water. Winter is for conserving energy and life, and its symbol is water.

The Five Elements symbolize the cycle of the five seasons summarized in the diagram on the right.

Hangeul is the most efficient phonemic writing system for all sounds of nature. Both Yin-Yang and the Five Elements are the basis for the sounds and the shapes of Hangeul, especially Yin-Yang for the vowels and the Five Elements for the consonants.

The Five Elements

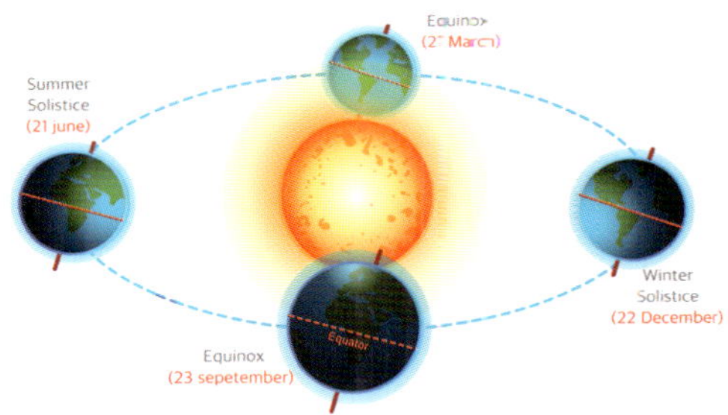

Revolution of the earth around the sun

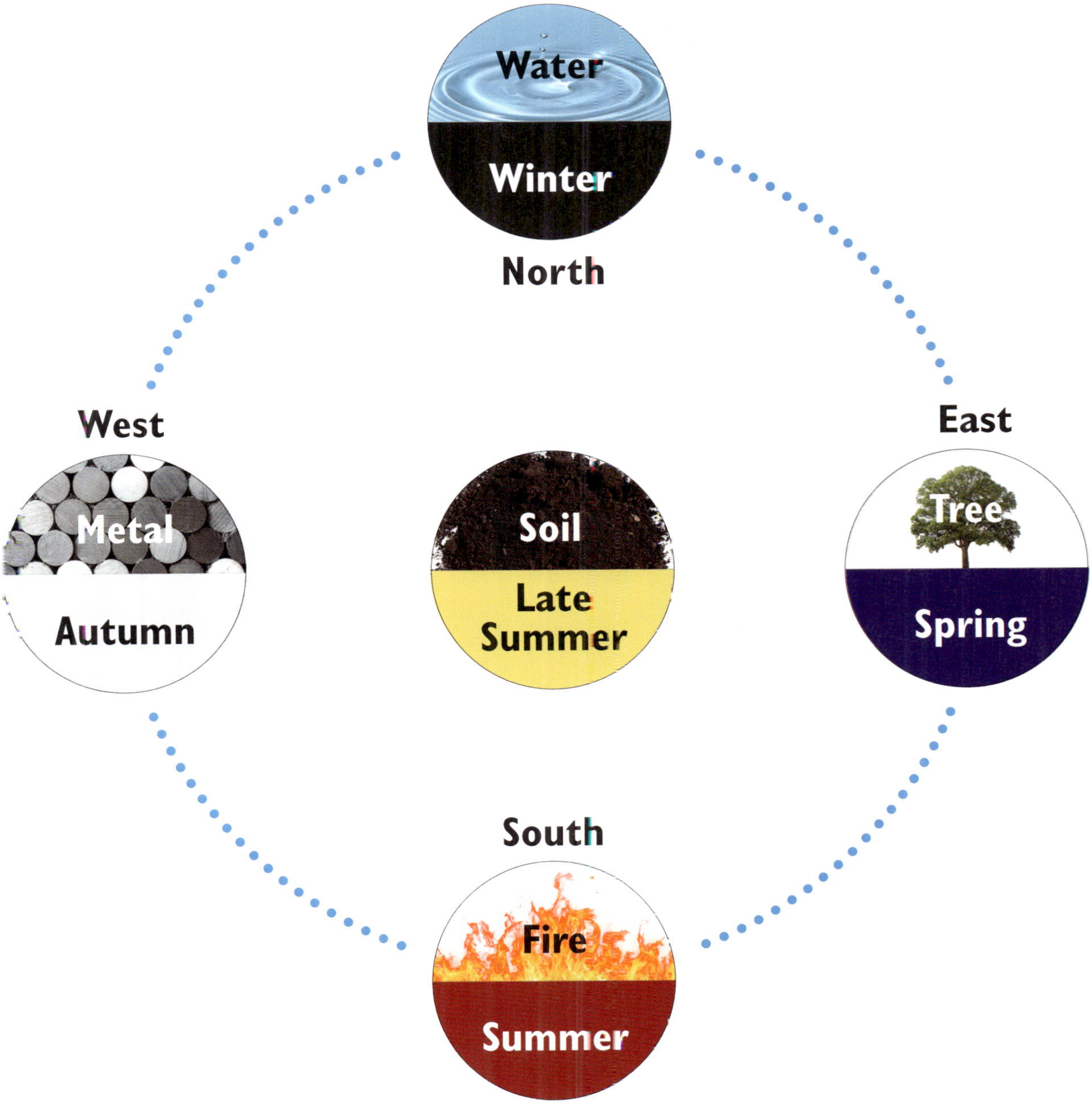

Contents

Prologue 4

Hangeul, characters for all the sounds of nature   4
The creation of Hangeul   5
The purpose of the invention of Hunminjeongeum   6
The fundamental principles of Hunminjeongeum   7

Vowels and Consonants of Hunminjeongeum and Hangeul 15

Vowels of Hunminjeongeum   16
Vowels of Hangeul   17
Consonants of Hunminjeongeum   18
Consonants of Hangeul   19

Vowels of Hangeul 21

Yin-Yang in the Vowels of Hangeul   22
Shall we start practicing writing vowels of Hangeul?   26

Consonants of Hangeul

39

The Five Elements in the Consonants of Hangeul   40
Shall we start practicing writing consonants of Hangeul?   46

Writing Hangeul as a Syllable

65

The Principles in Writing Hangeul as a Syllable   66
Syllable Writing Practice   68

Writing Practice of Hangeul Words

75

Appendix

119

Learning Hangeul using the Fingers   120
Places related to Hangeul   122

Vowels and Consonants of Hunminjeongeum and Hangeul

Vowels of Hunminjeongeum

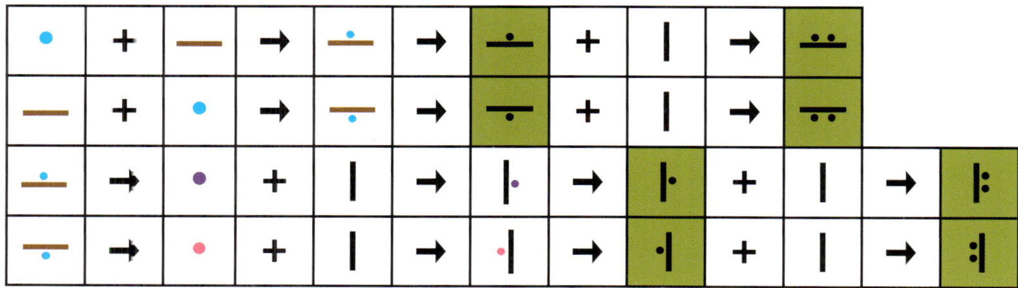

Original Korean alphabet,
Hunminjeongeum has a total of 29 vowels,
including 11 basic vowels and 18 complex
vowels.

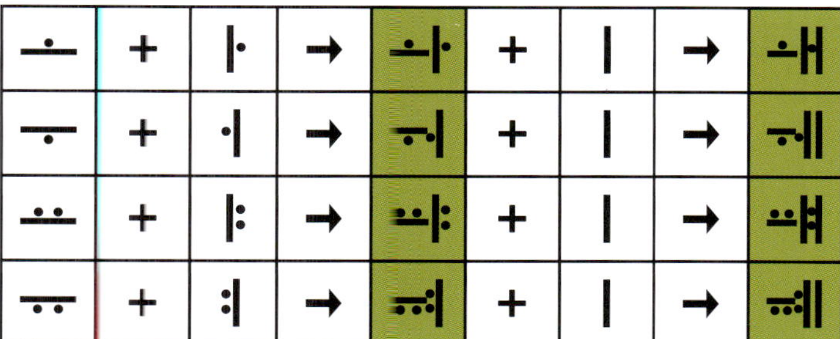

Vowels of Hangeul

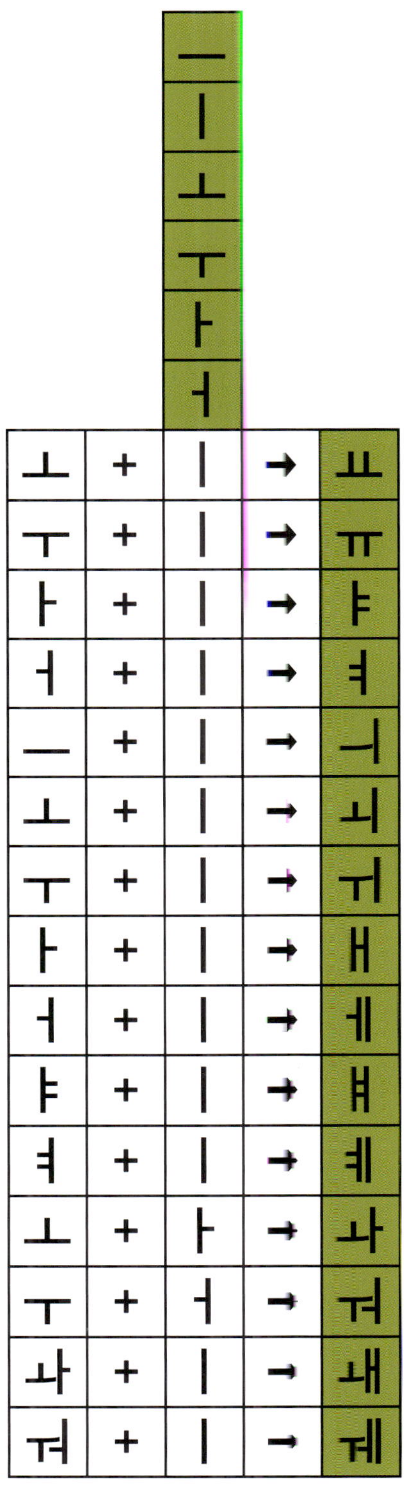

Modern Korean alphabet, Hangeul has a total of 21 vowels,
including 10 basic vowels and 11 diphthongs.

Consonants of Hunminjeongeum

Original Korean alphabet,
Hunminjeongeum has a total of 23 consonants, including
17 basic consonants and 6 strong consonants.

Consonants of Hangeul

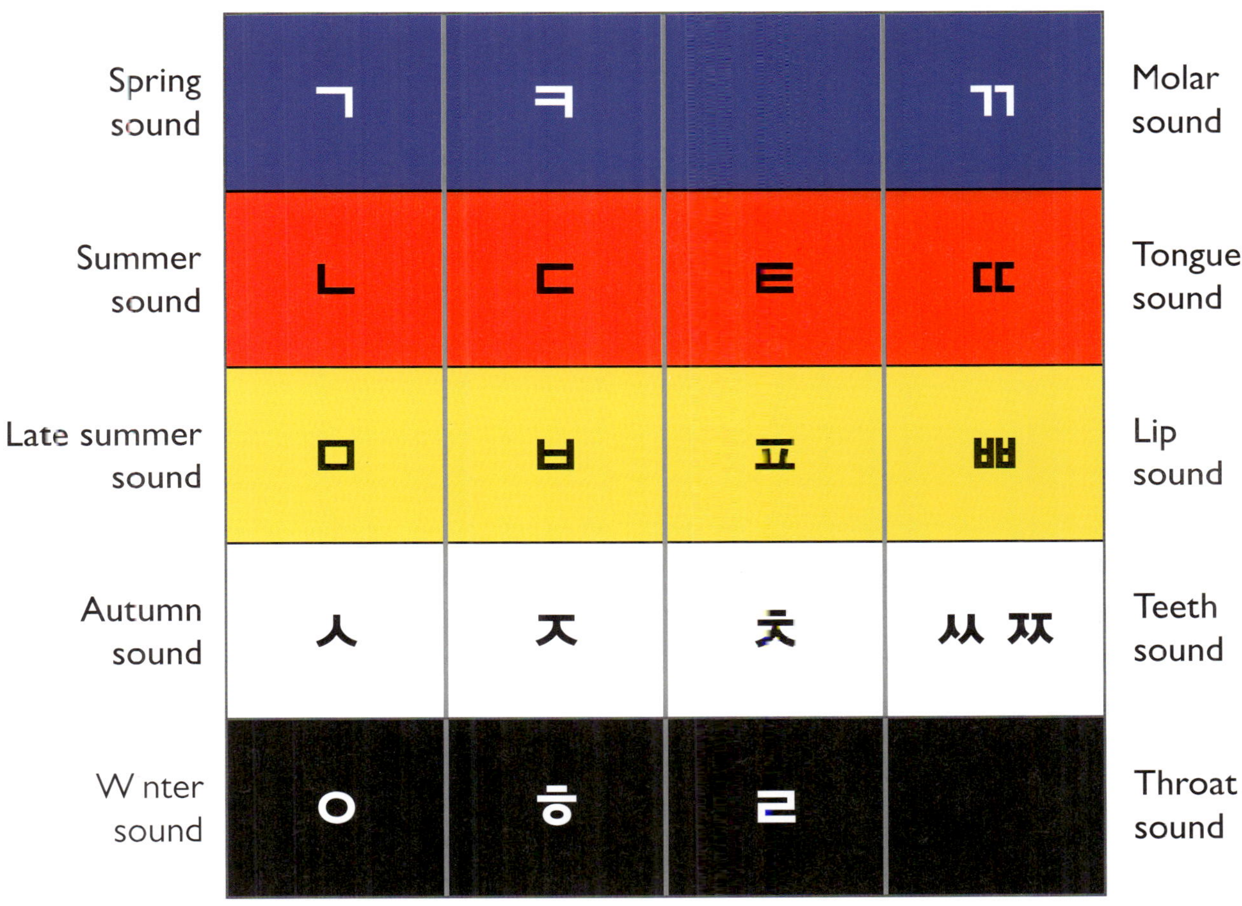

Modern Korean alphabet,
Hangeul has a total of 19 consonants, including
14 basic consonants and 5 strong consonants.

Vowels of Hangeul

Yin-Yang in the Vowels of Hangeul

Only an open mouth can make vowel sounds, not a closed mouth. Yin-Yang applies to the shapes and sounds of vowels by combining the sky sound, the earth sound and the human sound. Vowel sounds were created by pairing sounds generated by **retracting** or **stretching** the tongue and **closing** or **opening** the mouth.

Making vowel sounds is easiest when the mouth opens with the tongue in the middle of the mouth. In this position, one can generate other two basic vowels by retracting one's tongue toward the throat or stretching it toward the teeth. One can determine the order of these basic vowels according to the tongue's location and the depth of the sound. The relationship between this order and the major components of nature, the sky, the earth, and the human, is shown in the diagram. The shapes of three basic vowels symbolize the round sky (•), the flat earth (—) and the standing human (｜).

The basic vowels • , — , ｜ can combine to make more complicated vowels based on the Yin-Yang principle. The symbols for vowels are made by pairing the top and bottom and right and left together.

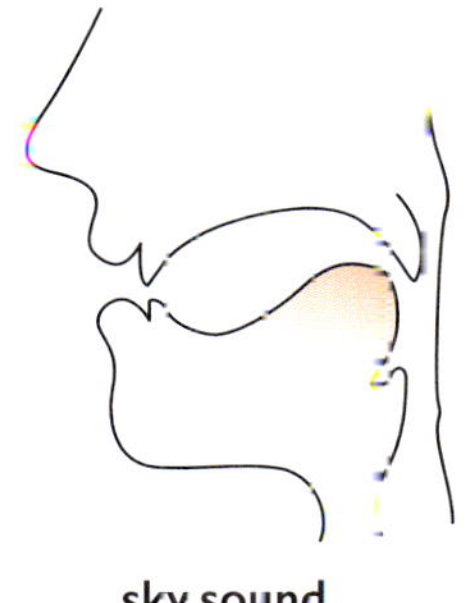

sky sound
(basic inward sound)

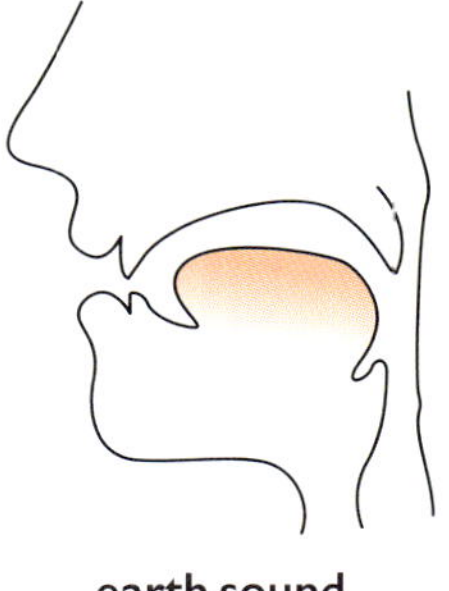

earth sound
(basic sound)

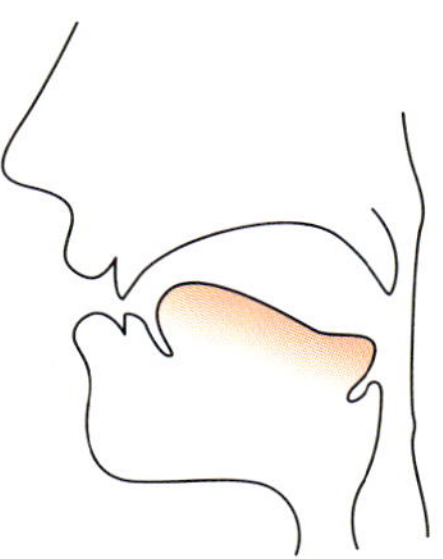

human sound
(basic outward sound)

When the sky sound is combined with the earth sound, the symbol of the vowel be-comes '⊥'. Today, '•' is expressed as a short line. Thus, '⊥' became '⊥'. This sound comes out when the lips are pursed with the tongue located in the sky sound position (inside). '⊥' sounds similar to [o] (so [s**o**u]).

The sound that comes out when the mouth opens with the tongue located in the sky sound position becomes '┣•', and '┣•' became '┣'. '┣' sounds similar to [a] (about [əb**a**ut]).

When the earth sound is combined with the sky sound, the symbol of the vowel be-comes '⊤'. Today, '⊤' became '⊤'. The lips make this sound when pursed with the tongue located in the earth sound position (middle). '⊤' sounds similar to [u] (so[so**u**]).

The sound that comes out when the mouth opens with the tongue located in the earth sound position becomes '•┤', and '•┤' became '┤'. '┤' sounds similar to [ə] (about [**ə**baut]).

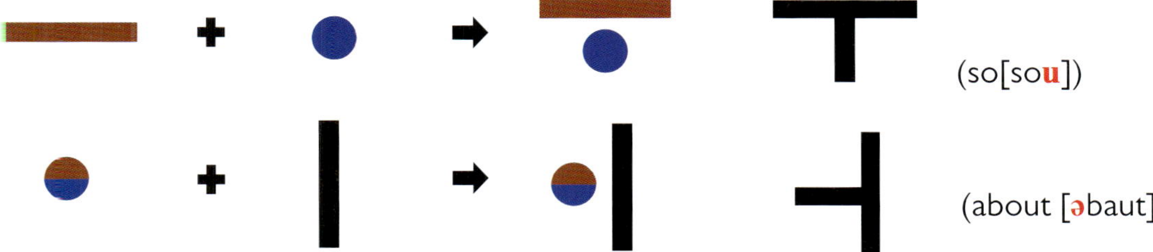

The pronunciation of both '⊥' and '𝜏' requires a closed mouth and is written with a shared '—'. '⊥' has an upward vertical line, while '𝜏' has a downward vertical line. Thus, '⊥' and '𝜏' are paired as 'top and bottom'.

Both 'ㅏ' and 'ㅓ' require one's mouth to be opened when they are pronounced, and share 'ㅣ' when they are written. 'ㅏ' has a horizontal line on the right, while 'ㅓ' has a horizontal line on the left. Thus 'ㅏ' and 'ㅓ' are paired as 'right and left'.

When the human sound 'ㅣ' is combined with the '⊥' sound, the symbol of the vowe becomes 'ㅛ'. The 'ㅛ' sounds similar to [jo].

When the human sound 'ㅣ' is combined with the '𝜏' sound, the symbol of the vowel becomes 'ㅠ'. The 'ㅠ' sounds similar to [ju].

When the human sound 'ㅣ' is combined with the 'ㅏ' sound, the symbol of the vowel becomes 'ㅑ'. The 'ㅑ' sounds similar to [ja].

When the human sound 'ㅣ' is combined with the 'ㅓ' sound, the symbol of the vowel becomes 'ㅕ'. The 'ㅕ' sounds similar to [jə].

'ㅛ' and 'ㅠ' make a pair as 'top and bottom', just like '⊥' and '𝜏'.

'ㅑ' and 'ㅕ' make a pair as 'right and left', just like 'ㅏ' and 'ㅓ'.

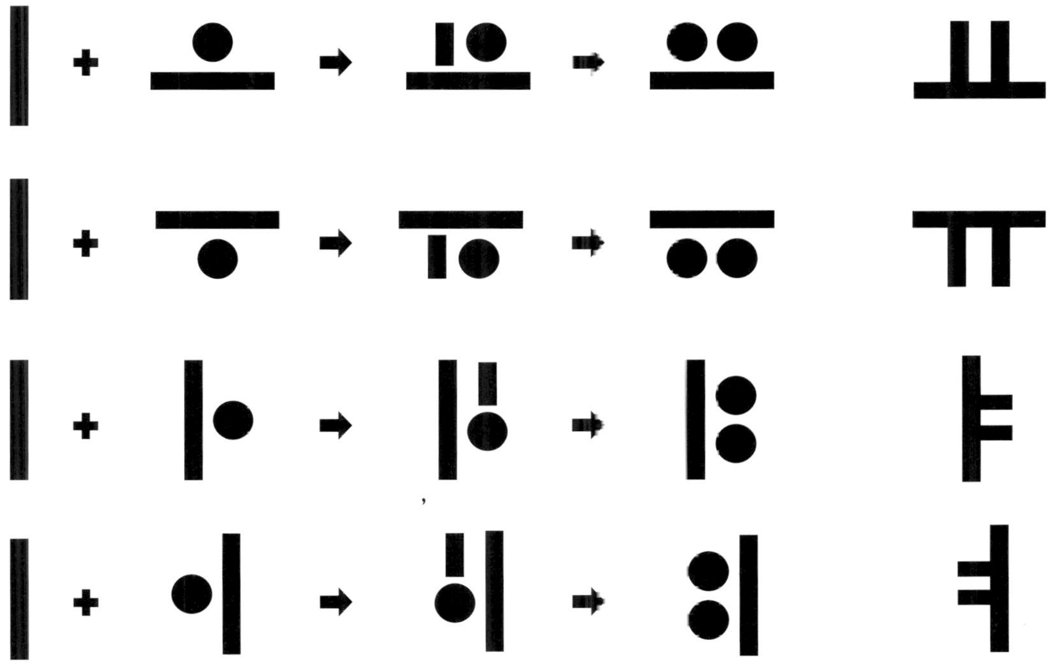

When '—', 'ㅗ', 'ㅜ', 'ㅏ', 'ㅓ', 'ㅑ', 'ㅕ' are combined with 'ㅣ', 'ㅢ', 'ㅚ', 'ㅟ', 'ㅐ', 'ㅔ', 'ㅒ', 'ㅖ' are made.

Yang characters can combine only with Yang characters. Thus, the combination of 'ㅗ' and 'ㅏ' makes 'ㅘ'.

Likewise, Yin characters can combine only with Yin characters. Thus, the combination of 'ㅜ' and 'ㅓ' makes 'ㅝ'.

When 'ㅘ' and 'ㅝ' are combined with 'ㅣ', 'ㅙ' and 'ㅞ' are made.

Shall we start practicing writing
vowels of Hangeul?

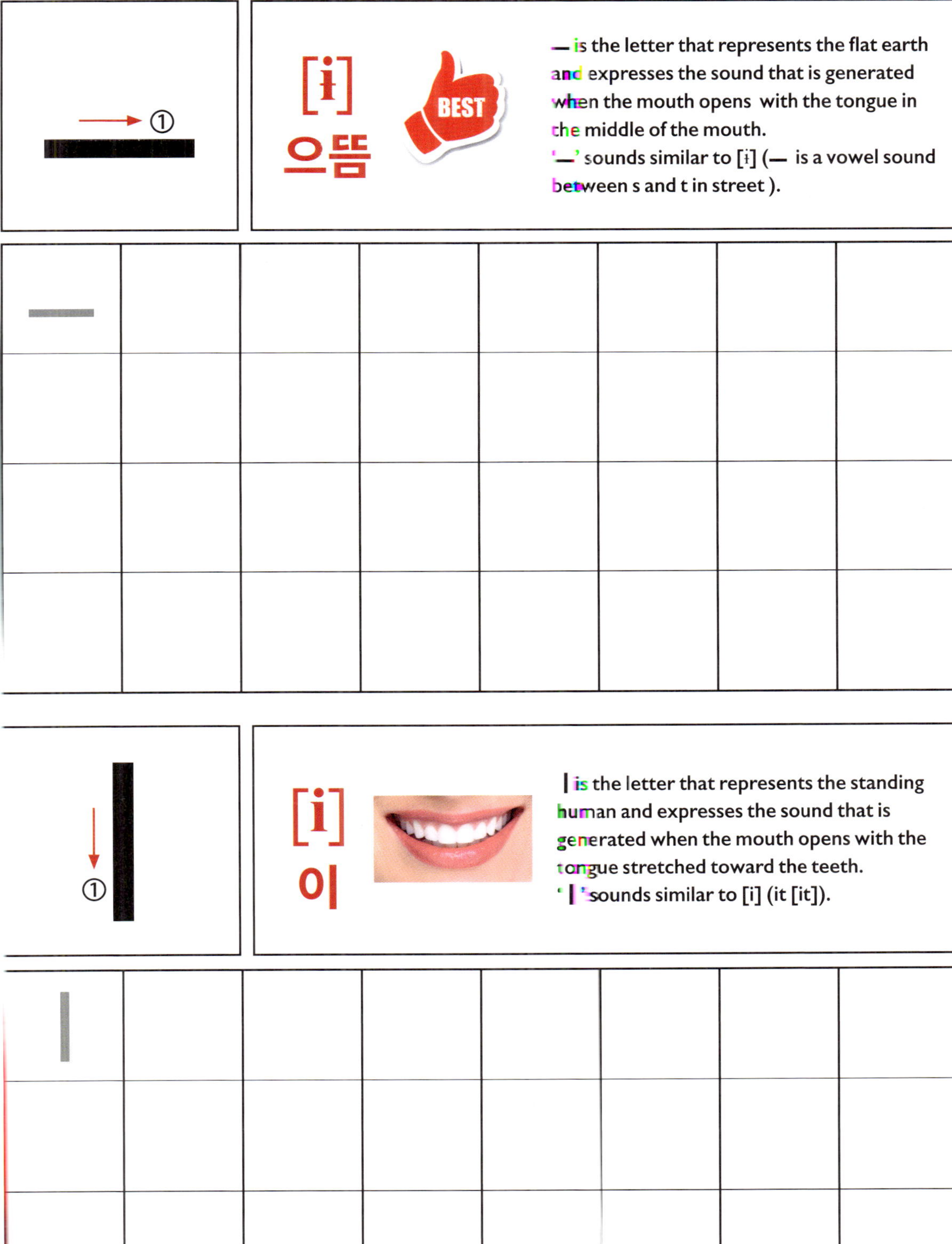

① ─

[i]
으뜸

BEST

— is the letter that represents the flat earth and expresses the sound that is generated when the mouth opens with the tongue in the middle of the mouth.
'—' sounds similar to [i] (— is a vowel sound between s and t in street).

[i]
이

| is the letter that represents the standing human and expresses the sound that is generated when the mouth opens with the tongue stretched toward the teeth.
'|' sounds similar to [i] (it [it]).

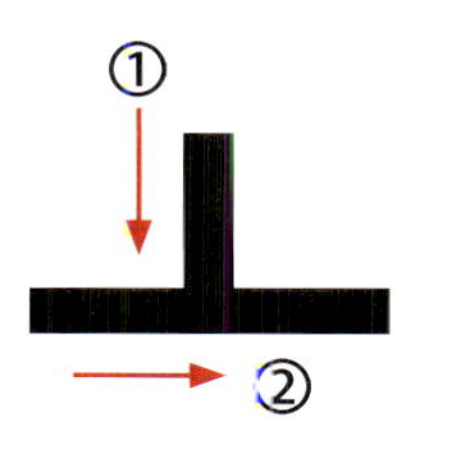

ㅗ is the letter that expresses the sound that comes out when the lips are pursed with the tongue retracting toward the throat. 'ㅗ' sounds similar to [o] (so [sou]).

ㅗ					

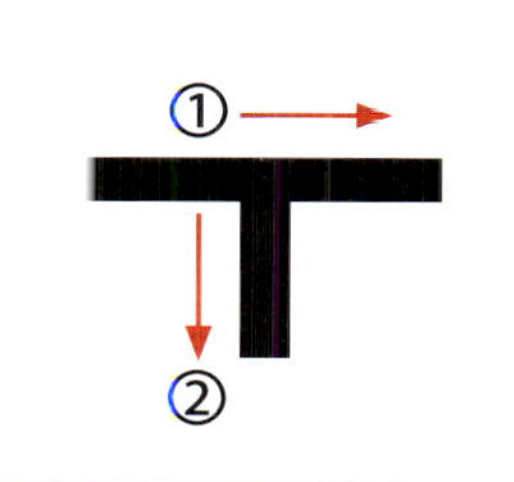

ㅜ is the letter that expresses the sound that comes out when the lips are pursed with the tongue located in the middle of the mouth. 'ㅜ' sounds similar to [u] (so[sou]).

ㅜ					

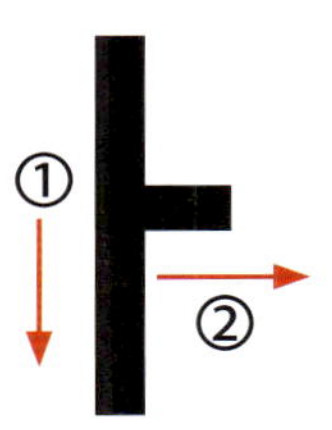

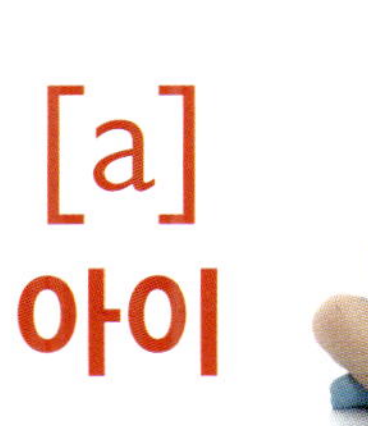

ㅏ is the letter that expresses the sound that comes out when the mouth opens when the tongue retracting toward the throat.
'ㅏ' sounds similar to [a] (about [əbaut]).

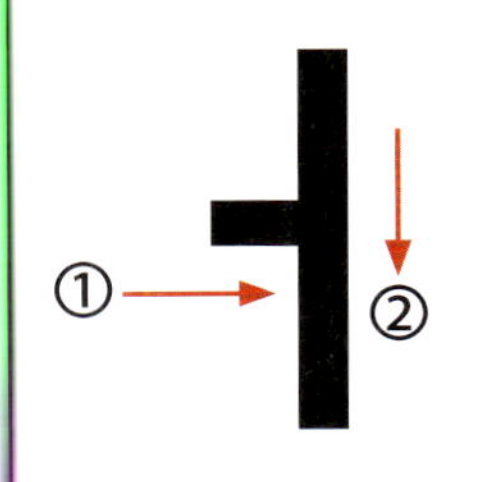

ㅓ is the letter that expresses the sound that comes out when the mouth opens when the tongue located in the middle of the mouth.
'ㅓ' sounds similar to [ə] (about [əbaut]).

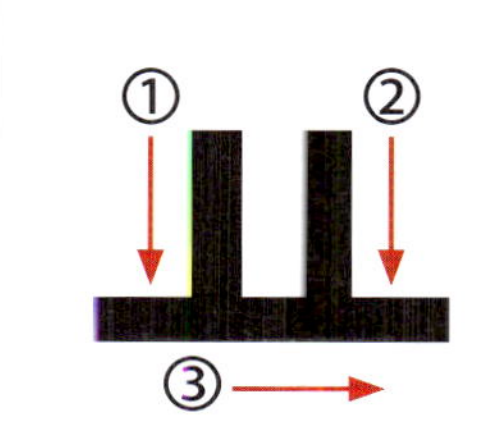

[jo]
요일

⠇⠇ is the letter that expresses the sound that is generated when ' ㅣ ' sound is followed by 'ㅗ' sound.

'ㅛ' sounds similar to [jo] (Yo Yo [jojo]).

ㅛ					

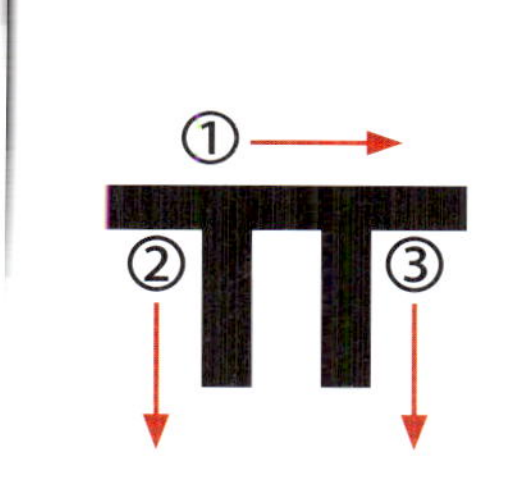

[ju]
유월

ㅠ is the letter that that expresses the sound that is generated when ' ㅣ ' sound is followed by 'ㅜ' sound.

'ㅠ' sounds similar to [ju] (you [ju]).

ㅠ					

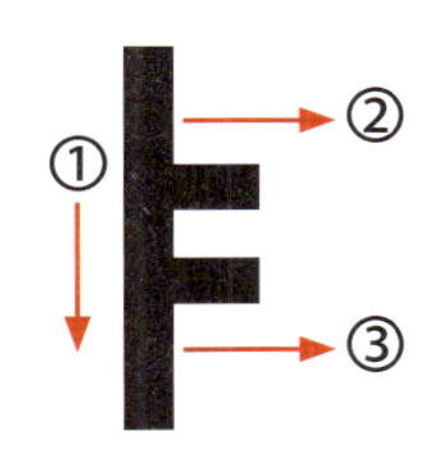

ㅑ is the letter that expresses the sound that is generated when 'ㅣ' sound is followed by 'ㅏ' sound.
'ㅑ' sounds similar to [ja] (yard [ja:rd]).

ㅑ						

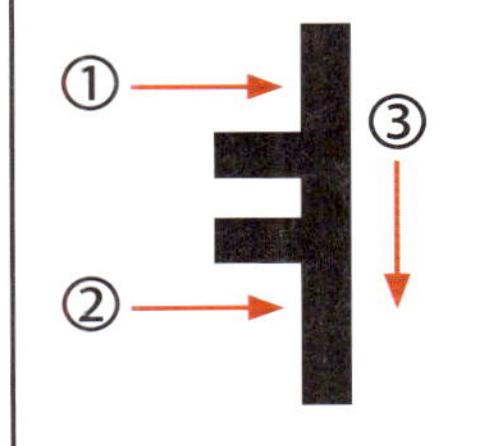

ㅕ is the letter that expresses the sound that is generated when 'ㅣ' sound is followed by 'ㅓ' sound.
'ㅕ' sounds similar to [jə] (yawn).

ㅕ						

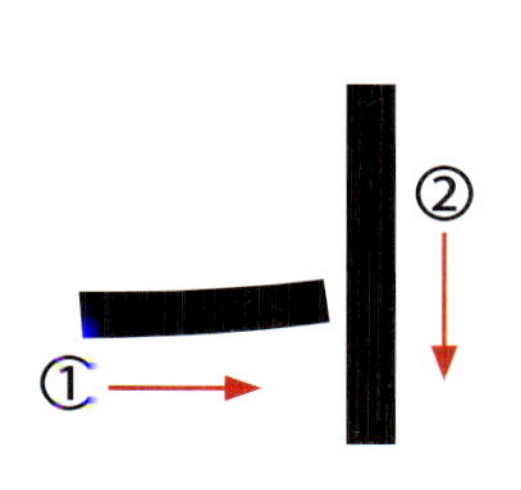

[ui]
의자

ㅢ is the letter that expresses the sound that is generated when the '—' sound is followed by ' | ' sound.
'ㅢ' sounds similar to [ui].

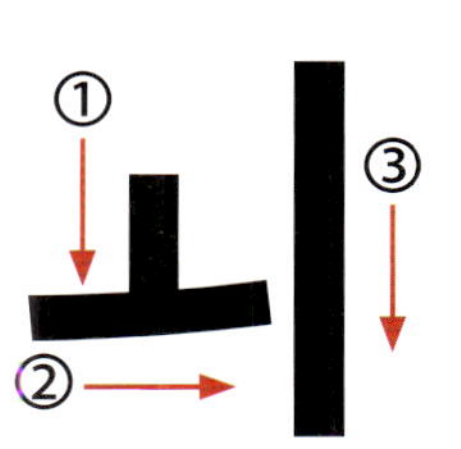

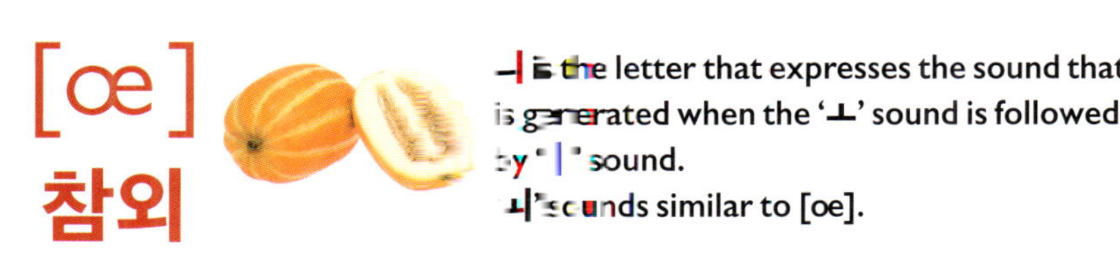

[œ]

참외

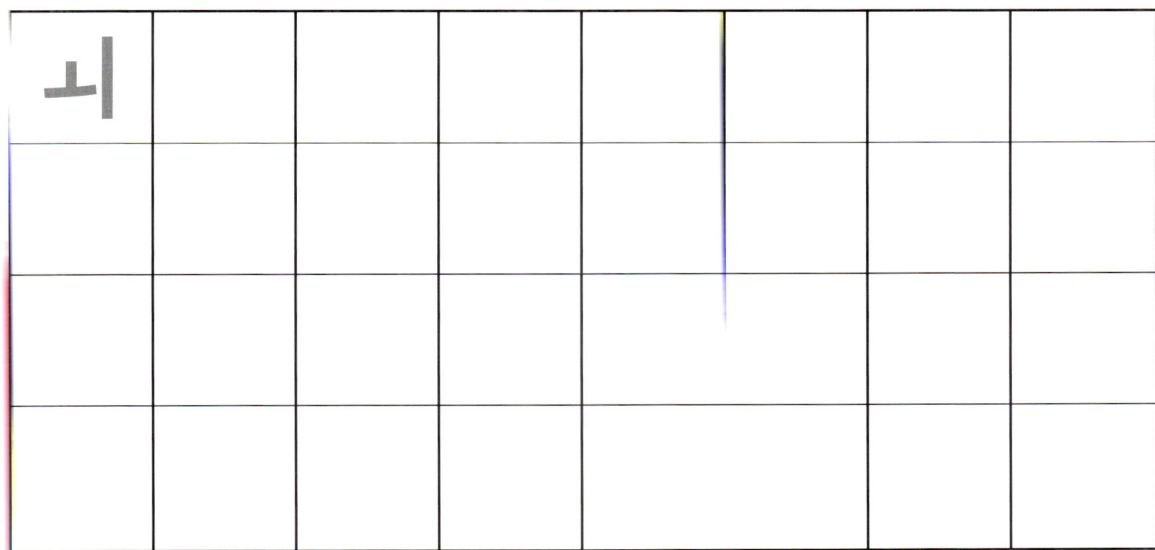

ㅚ is the letter that expresses the sound that is generated when the 'ㅗ' sound is followed by 'ㅣ' sound.
'ㅚ' sounds similar to [œ].

ㅚ						

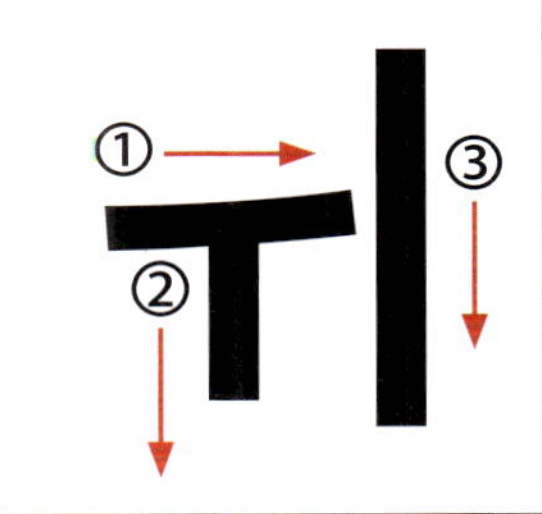

[wi]

위

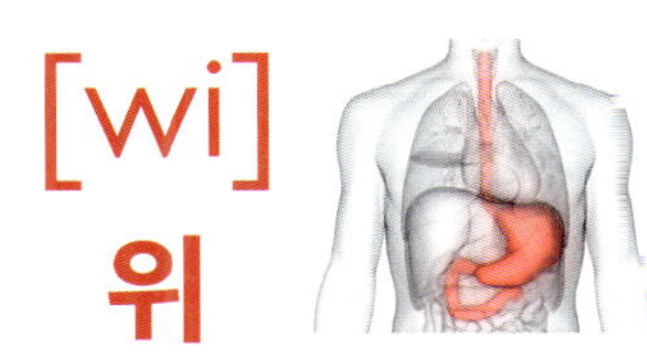

ㅟ is the letter that expresses the sound that is generated when the 'ㅜ' sound is followed by 'ㅣ' sound.
'ㅟ' sounds similar to [wi] (we [wi]).

ㅟ						

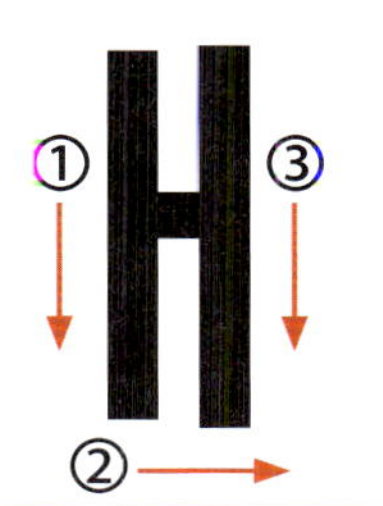

ㅐ is the letter that is made when ' ㅣ ' is combined with ㅏ.
' ㅐ ' sounds similar to [æ] (apple[æpl]).

ㅐ						

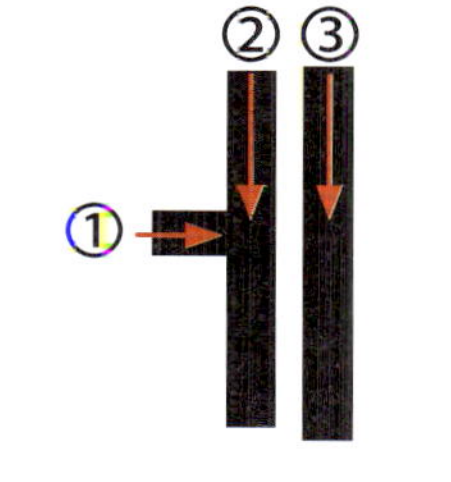

ㅔ is the letter that is made when ' ㅣ ' is combined with ㅓ.
' ㅔ ' sounds similar to [e] (every [evri]).

ㅔ						

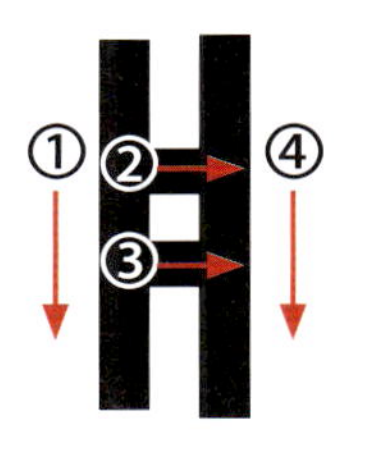

ㅐ is the letter that expresses the sound that is generated when 'ㅣ' sound is followed by 'ㅏ' sound.
'ㅐ' sounds similar to [jæ](yankee [jænki]).

ㅐ						

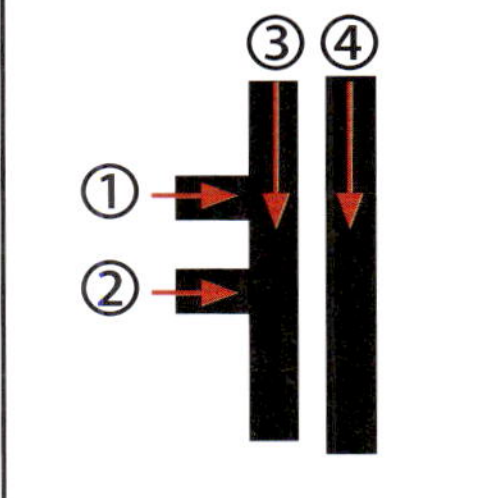

ㅖ is the letter that expresses the sound that is generated when 'ㅣ' sound is followed by 'ㅓ' sound.
'ㅖ' sounds similar to [je] (yes [jes]).

ㅖ						

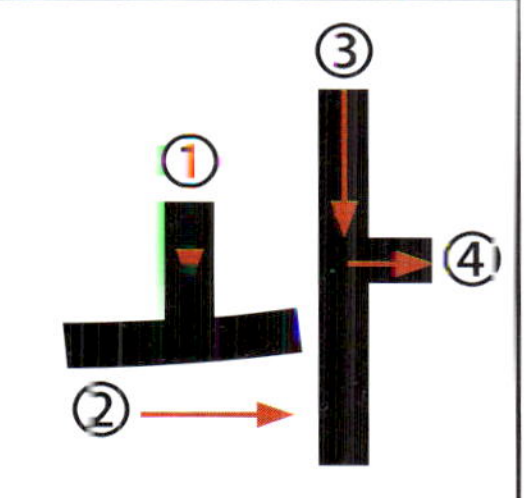

[wa]
기와

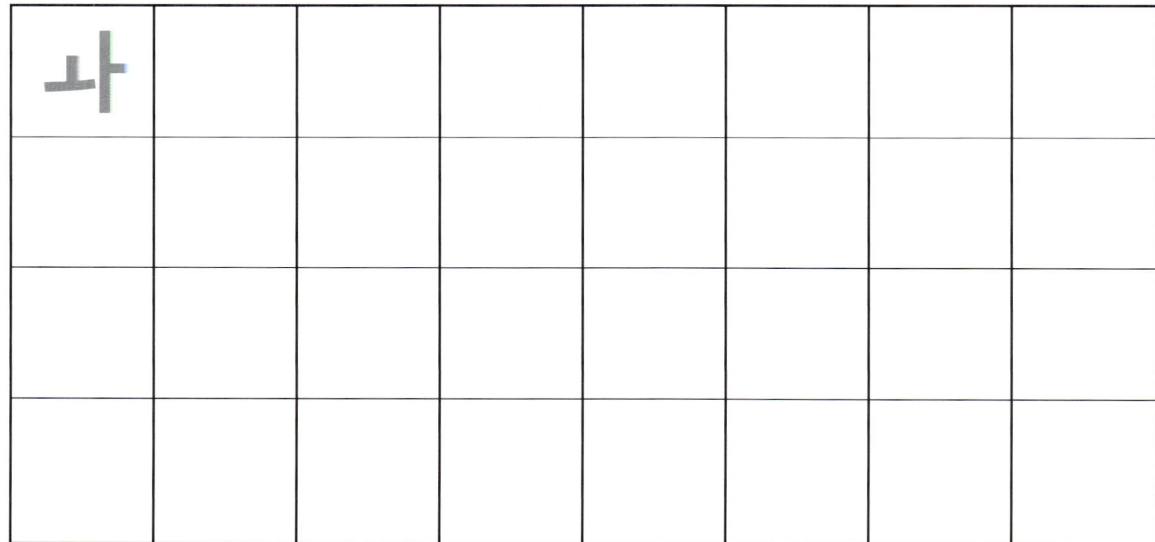

ᅪ is the letter that expresses the sound that is generated when the 'ㅗ' sound is followed by 'ㅏ' sound.

'ᅪ' sounds similar to [wa] (what[wat]).

ᅪ

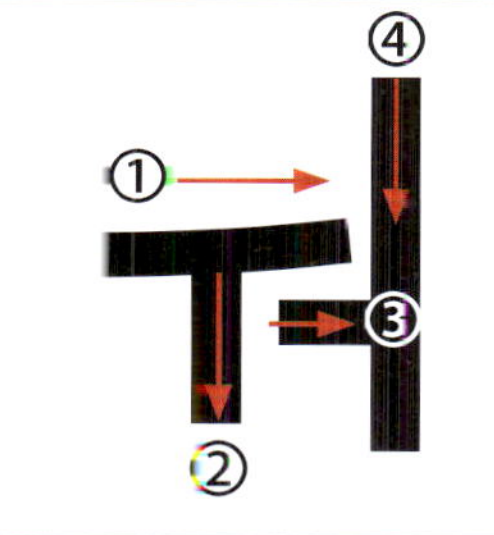

[wə]
워터

ᅯ is the letter that expresses the sound that is generated when the 'ㅜ' sound is followed by 'ㅓ' sound.

'ᅯ' sounds similar to [wə] (worry[wəri]).

ᅯ

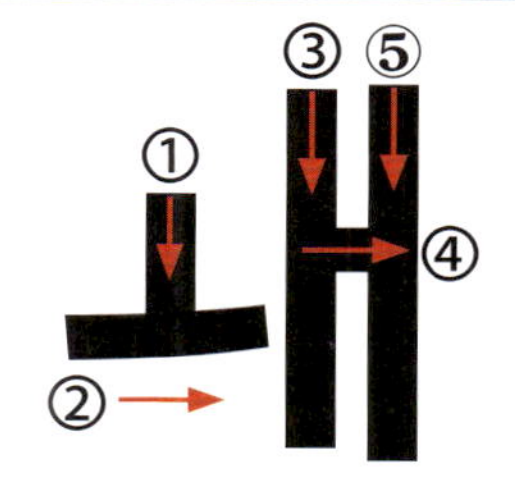

[wæ]

왜

ㅙ is the letter that is made when 'ㅣ' is combined with ㅚ.
'ㅙ' sounds similar to [wæ] (wagon [wægən]).

ㅙ						

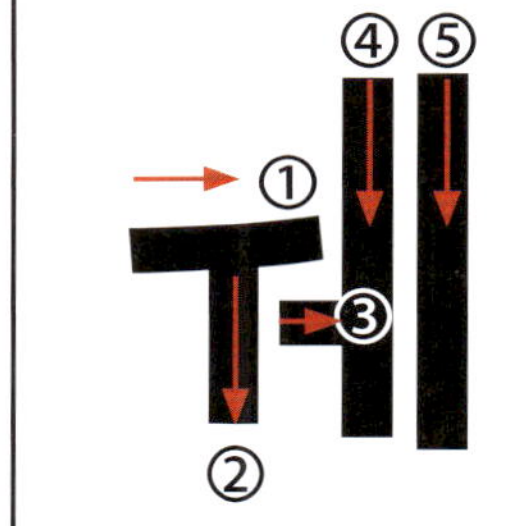

[we]

웨이터

ㅞ is the letter that is made when 'ㅣ' is combined with ㅝ
'ㅞ' sounds similar to [we] (way [wei]).

ㅞ						

Consonants of Hangeul

The Five Elements in the Consonants of Hangeul

Five sites generate the basic consonants; the inner throat, the molars, the tongue attached to the palate, the outer lips, and the teeth inside the mouth. The properties of each sound and each position of the vocal organs match up with each of the five seasons, leading to such pairings.

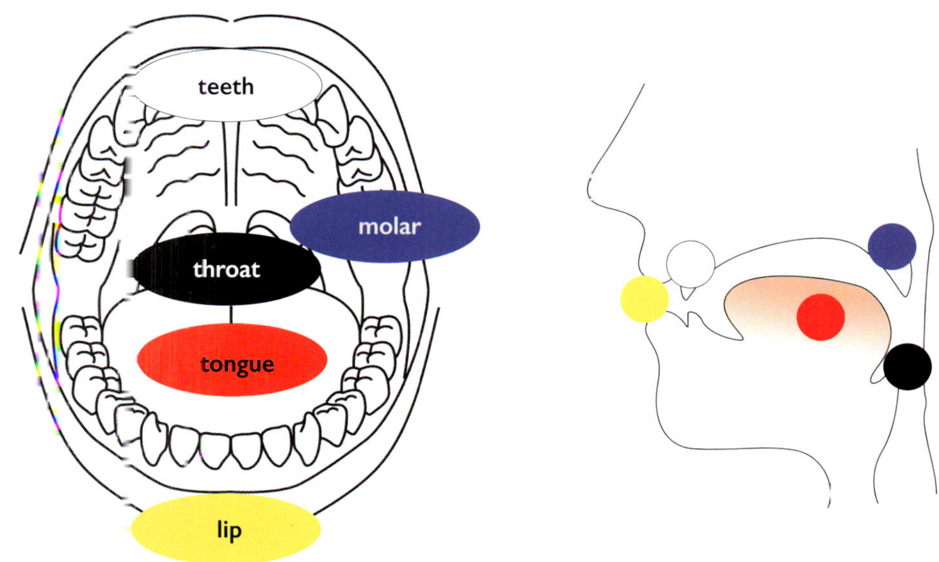

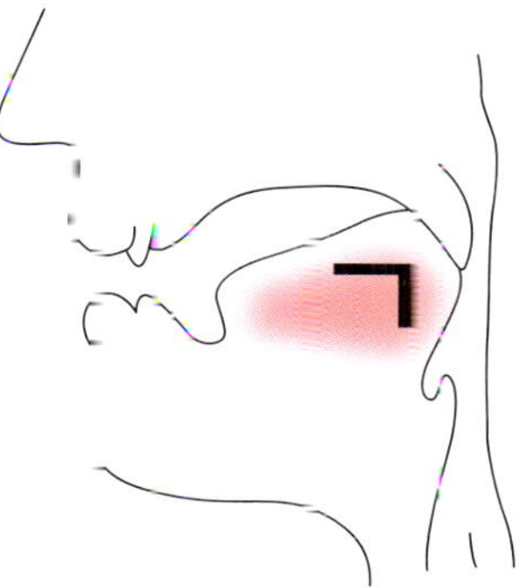

The sound corresponding to spring is the molar sound, generated when the tongue touches the molars and closes the throat. The molar sound is similar to but more "ripened" than the throat sound, just like a tree in spring. Therefore, it is classified as the sound of spring. ㄱ is the letter that expresses the sound [g] as in 'again', made when the throat is closed by the tongue at the molars. The side view of the tongue making the 'ㄱ' sound enables us to imagine the shape of ㄱ.

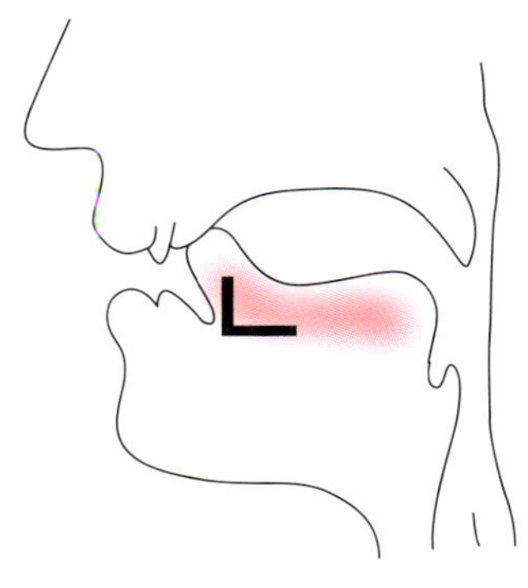

The sound corresponding to summer is the tongue sound, generated when the tongue touches the palate and then drops down quickly. The tongue is sharp and mobile, so the tongue sound rolls and darts in and out like a blazing fire. This similarity may be the reason why the tongue sound is called the sound of summer. ㄴ is the letter expressing the sound [n] as in 'need', made when the tongue touches the palate. If we could see the figure of the tongue from the side, we could imagine the shape of ㄴ.

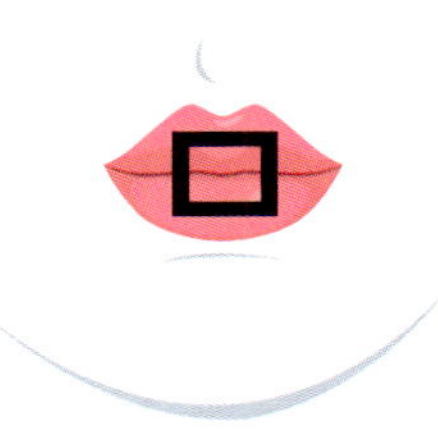

The sound corresponding to late summer is the lip sound, generated when the lips put on and off together. The sound remains inside the mouth, like soil preserving the many lives inside of it. ㅁ is the letter that expresses the sound [m] as in 'moon', made by putting the two lips on and off together. The shape of the closed mouth from the front reminds us of the character ㅁ.

The sound corresponding to the fall is the teeth sound, generated when the upper and lower teeth touch each other. Since the teeth are stout and able to cut everything, King Sejong compared them to metal. ㅅ is the letter that expresses the sound [s] as in 'smile', which comes out when the upper and lower teeth are in contact. The shape of ㅅ resembles the teeth engaging with each other.

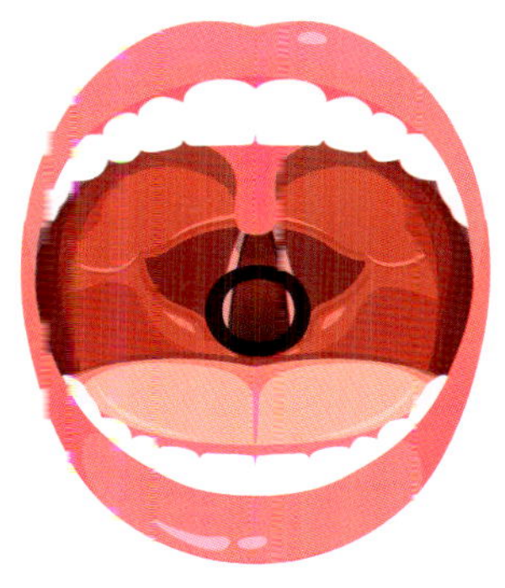

The sound corresponding to winter is the throat sound that comes out when the throat is fully open. Since the throat is always wet, it can be comparable to water. ㅇ is the letter that expresses the sound generated in the throat. The image of the throat reminds us of the shape of ㅇ. ㅇ represents two sounds. When ㅇ comes at the beginning of a syllable, it doesn't have any sound while the throat is open. But when ㅇ comes at the end of a syllable after a vowel, it represents the same sound [ŋ] as in 'king' while the throat is closed off.

ㄹ expresses two different sounds as well. When it comes to the first consonant, it sounds similar to [r]. When it comes to the final consonant, however, it sounds similar to [l].

Adding a horizontal bar to the basic consonant letters makes the characters for harder sounds:

ㅋ is the letter made by adding a bar to ㄱ and expresses a harder sound than ㄱ with the same position of the tongue at the molars as ㄱ. ㅋ expresses the sound [k] as in 'cut'.

ㄷ is the letter made by adding a bar to ㄴ and expresses a harder sound than ㄴ with the same position of the tongue on the palate as ㄴ. ㄷ expresses the sound [d] as in 'deed'.
Adding a bar to ㄷ forms the letter ㅌ, which expresses a harder sound than ㄷ. ㅌ expresses the sound [t] as in 'tea'.

ㅂ is the letter made by adding two short bars to the top of ㅁ and expresses a harder sound than ㅁ with the same position of the mouth as ㅁ. ㅂ expresses the sound [b] as in 'book'.

ㅍ is the letter made by adding four short bars to the right and the left of ㅁ and expresses a harder sound than ㅂ. ㅍ expresses the sound [p] as in 'police' .

ㅈ is the letter made by adding a bar to ㅅ and expresses a harder sound than ㅅ with the same position of the teeth as ㅅ. ㅈ expresses the sound [dʒ] as in 'judge'.

Adding a bar to ㅈ forms the letter ㅊ, which expresses a harder sound than ㅈ. ㅊ expresses the sound [ts] as in 'child'.

ㆆ is the letter made by adding a bar to ㅇ, which is not used now.

Adding a bar to ㆆ forms the letter ㅎ, which expresses a harder sound than ㆆ. ㅎ expresses the sound [h] as in 'head'.

Putting two identical consonants together creates the letters for stronger fortis sounds. These sounds are somewhat unique to the Korean language

ㄱ + ㄱ = ㄲ [k´] as in 깨 (sesame seed)

ㄷ + ㄷ = ㄸ [t´] as in 딸 (daughter)

ㅂ + ㅂ = ㅃ [p´] as in 빵 (bread)

ㅅ + ㅅ = ㅆ [s´] as in 쌀 (rice)

ㅈ + ㅈ = ㅉ [tʃ´] as in 짠 (salty)

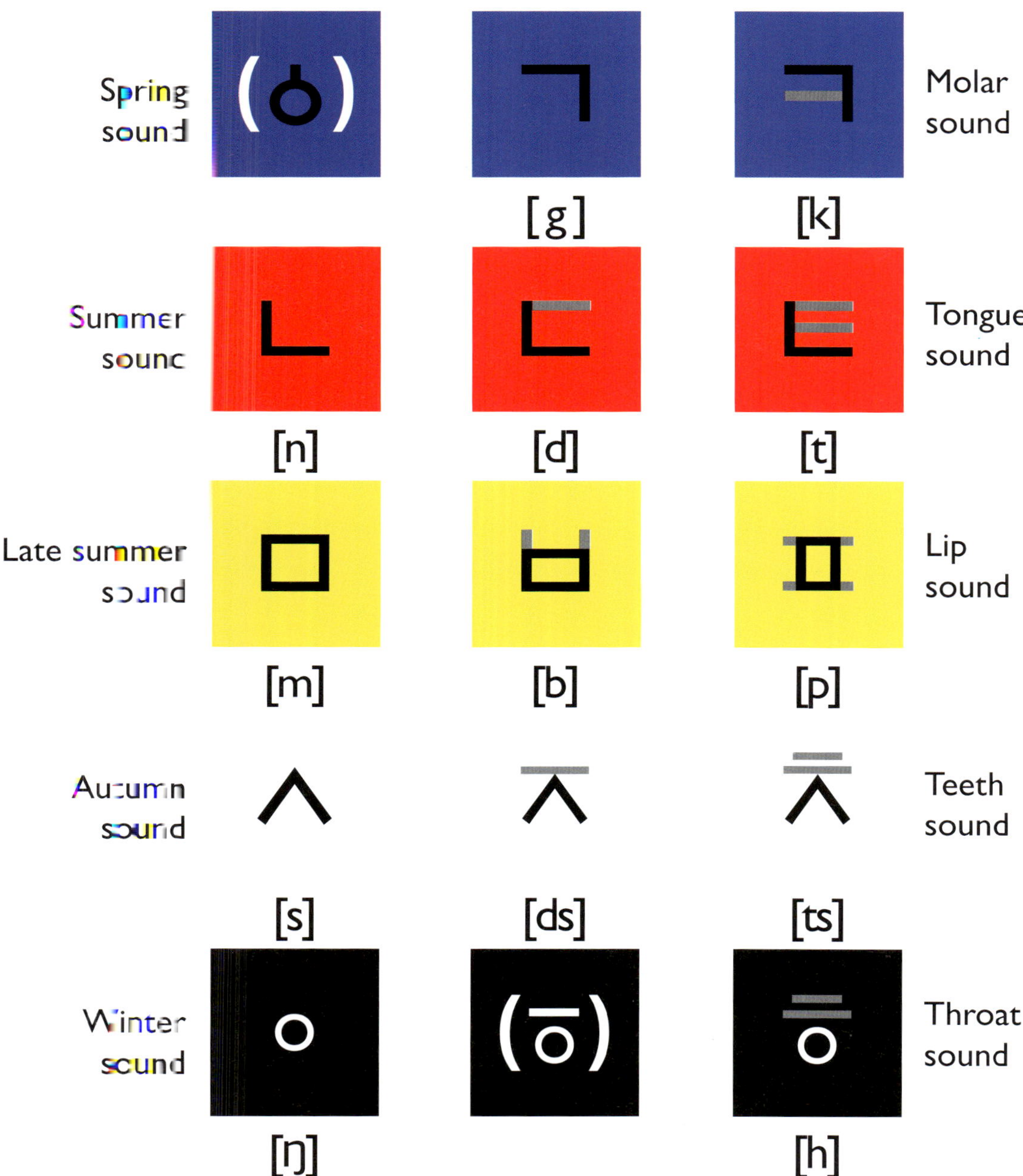

Spring sound
Molar sound
[g]
[k]
Summer sound
Tongue sound
[n]
[d]
[t]
Late summer sound
Lip sound
[m]
[b]
[p]
Autumn sound
Teeth sound
[s]
[ds]
[ts]
Winter sound
Throat sound
[ŋ]
[h]

I
한 글
(HANGEUL)

Shall we start practicing writing

consonants of Hangeul?

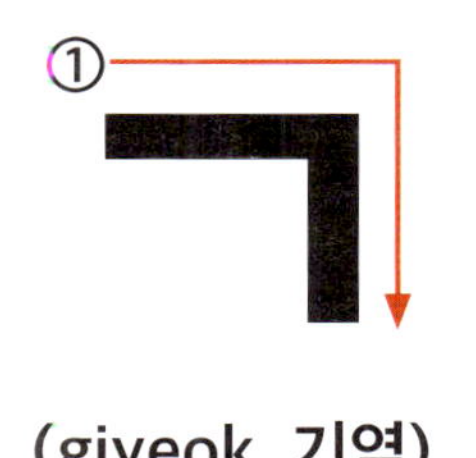
(giyeok, 기역)

[g]
구두

ㄱ is the letter that expresses the sound [g] as in 'again', generated when the throat is closed by the tongue at the molars. The side view of the tongue making the 'ㄱ' sound enables us to imagine the shape of ㄱ.

ㄱ

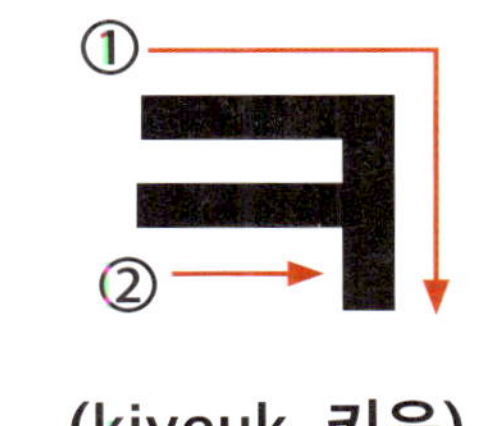
(kiyeuk, 키윽)

[k]
코끼리

ㅋ is the letter made by adding a bar to ㄱ and expresses a harder sound than ㄱ with the same position of the tongue at the molars as ㄱ. ㅋ expresses the sound [k] as in 'cut'.

ㅋ

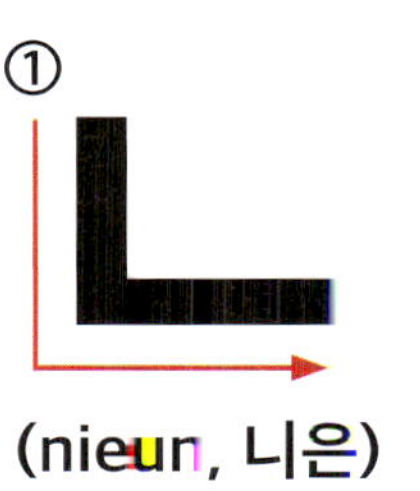

① **ㄴ**

(nieun, 니은)

[n]
나비

ㄴ is the letter expressing the sound [n] as in 'need', made when the tongue touches the palate. If we could see the figure of the tongue from the side, we could imagine the shape of ㄴ.

ㄴ

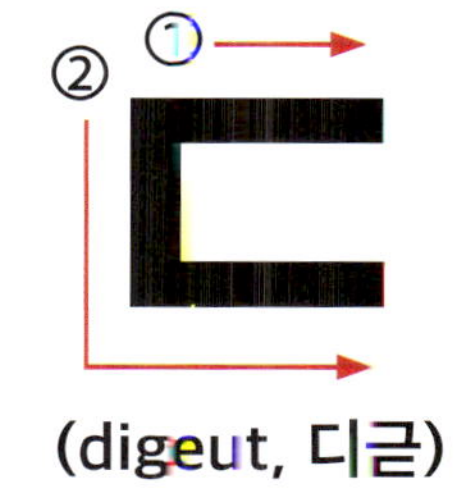

② **ㄷ**

(digeut, 디귿)

[d]
도자기

ㄷ is the letter made by adding a bar to ㄴ and expresses a harder sound than ㄴ with the same position of the tongue on the palate as ㄴ. ㄷ expresses the sound [d] as in 'deed'.

ㄷ

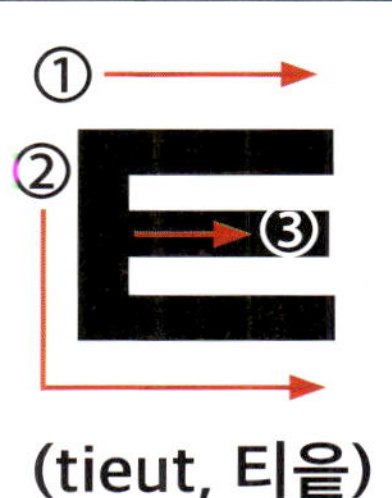

(tieut, 티읕)

[t]
태극기

ㅌ is the letter made by adding a bar to ㄷ and expresses a harder sound than ㄷ with the same position of the tongue on the palate as ㄴ. ㅌ expresses the sound [t] as in 'tea'.

ㅌ

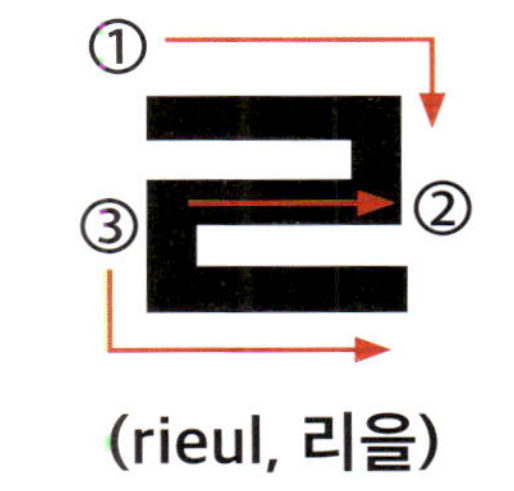

(rieul, 리을)

[l]
라면

ㄹ expresses two different sounds. When it comes to the first consonant, it sounds similar to [r]. When it comes to the final consonant, it sounds similar to [l].

ㄹ

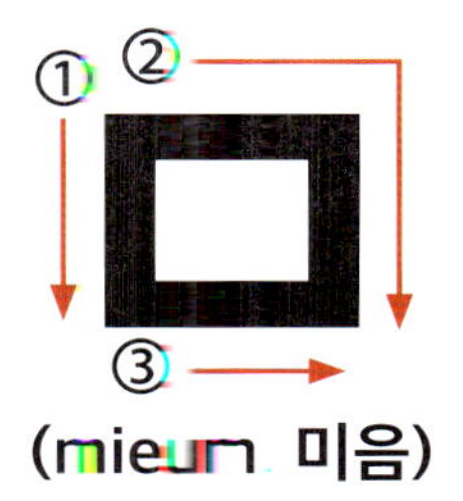

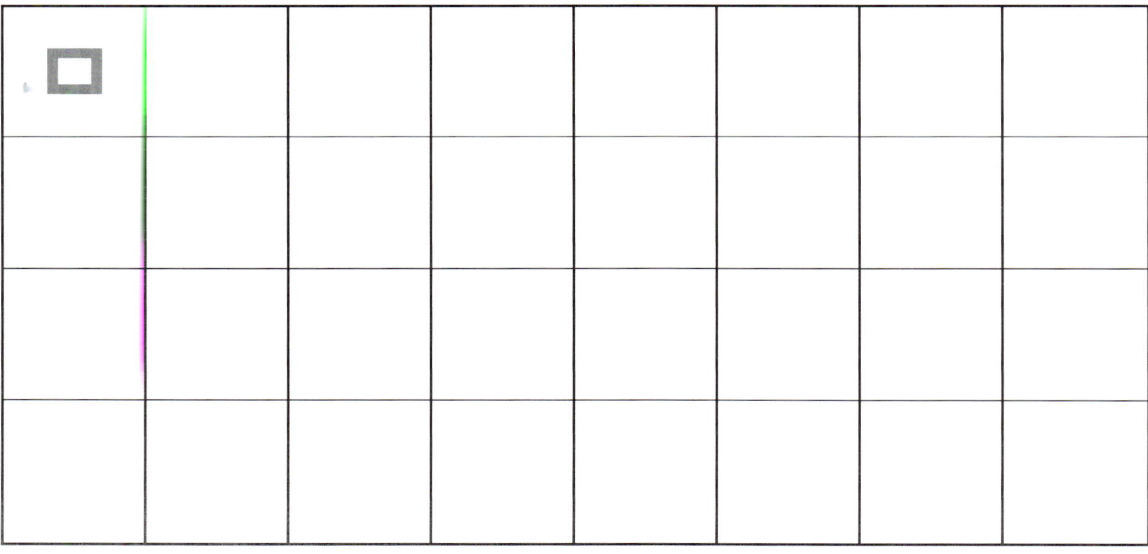

口 is the letter that expresses the sound [m] as in 'moon' made by putting the two lips on and off together. The shape of the closed mouth from the front reminds us the shape of 口.

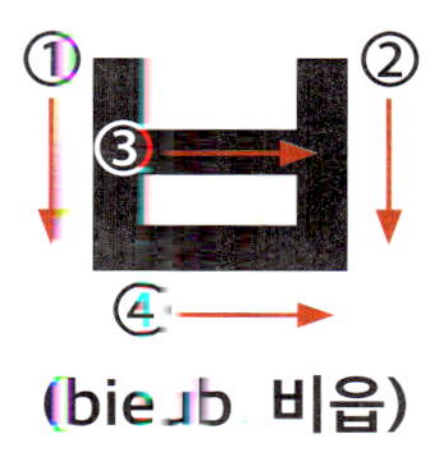

ㅂ is the letter made by adding two short bars to the top of 口 and expresses a harder sound than 口 with the same position of the mouth as 口. ㅂ expresses the sound [b] as in 'book'.

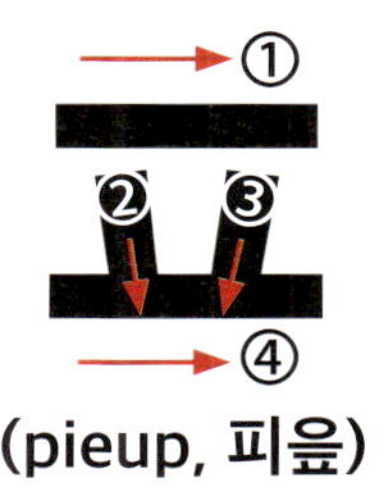

(pieup, 피읕)

[p]

포도

ㅍ is the letter made by adding four short bars to the right and the left of ㅁ and expresses a harder sound than ㅂ with the same position of the mouth as ㅂ. ㅍ expresses the sound [p] as in 'police'

ㅍ						

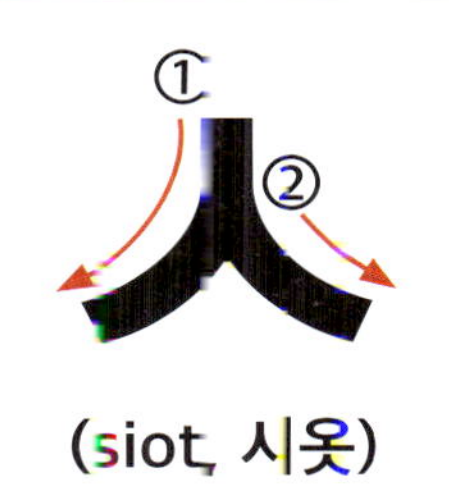

(siot, 시옷)

[s]
새

ㅅ is the letter that expresses the sound [s] as in 'smile', which comes out when the upper and lower teeth are in contact. The shape of ㅅ resembles the teeth engaging with each other.

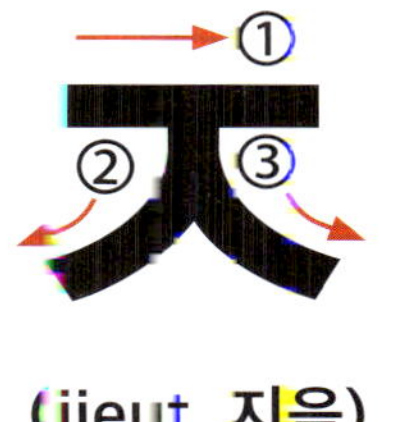

(jieut, 지읒)

[ds]
자동차

ㅈ is the letter made by adding a bar to ㅅ and expresses a harder sound than ㅅ with the same position of the teeth as ㅅ. ㅈ expresses the sound [dz] as in 'judge'.

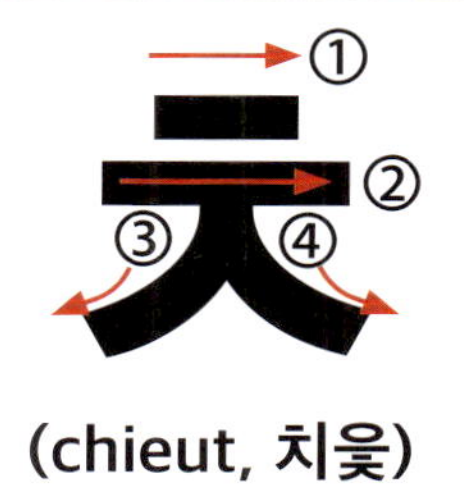

(chieut, 치읓)

[ts]

치약

ㅊ is the letter made by adding a bar to ㅈ and expresses a harder sound than ㅈ with the same position of the teeth as ㅅ. ㅊ expresses the sound [ts] as in 'child'.

ㅊ							

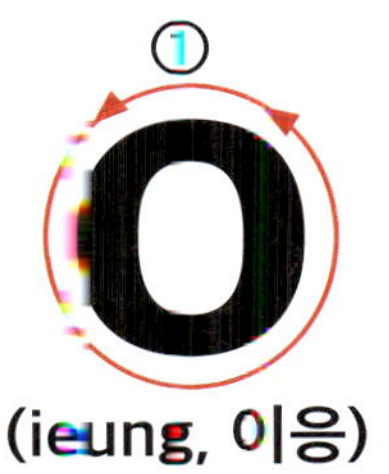

(ieung, 이응)

[ŋ]
안경

ㅇ is the letter that expresses the sound generated in the throat. The image of the throat reminds us the shape of **ㅇ** .
ㅇ expresses two sounds. When o comes at the beginning of a syllable, **ㅇ** doesn't have any sound while the throat is open. But when **ㅇ** comes at the end of a syllable after a vowel, it represents the sound [ŋ] as in 'king' while the throat is closed off.

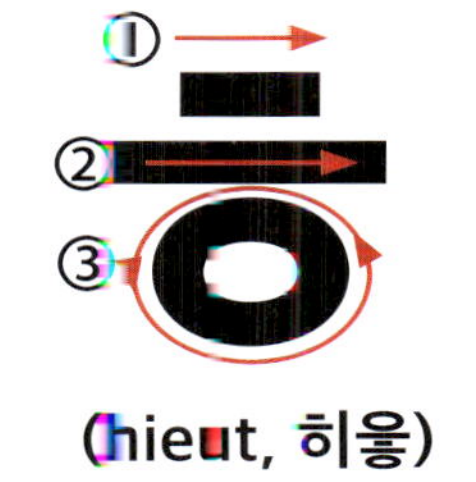

(hieut, 히읗)

[h]
한복

ㅎ is the letter by adding a bar to ㆆ that is not used now and expresses a harder sound than ㆆ. ㅎ expresses the sound [h] as in 'head'.

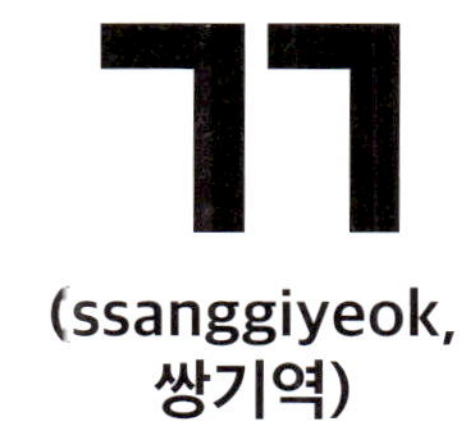

ㄲ

(ssanggiyeok,
쌍기역)

[k´]

꽃

ㄲ is the letter the stronger fortis sound of 'ㄱ' sound. This letter is made by putting two ㄱs together. This sound is somewhat unique to Korean.

ㄲ

ㄸ

(ssangdigeut,
쌍디귿)

[t´]

딸기

ㄸ is the letter for stronger fortis sound of 'ㄷ' sound. This letter is made by putting two ㄷs together. This sound is somewhat unique to Korean.

ㄸ

(ssangbieub, 쌍비읍)

ㅃ is the letter for stronger fortis sound of 'ㅂ' sound. This letter is made by putting two ㅂs together. This sound is somewhat unique to Korean.

ㅃ						

(ssangsiot, 쌍시옷)

ㅆ is the letter for stronger fortis sound of 'ㅅ' sound. This letter is made by putting two ㅅs together. This sound is somewhat unique to Korean.

ㅆ						

ㅉ

(ssangjieut, 쌍지읒)

[tʃ´]

짜장면

ㅉ is the letter for stronger fortis sound of 'ㅈ' sound. This letter is made by putting two ㅈ's together. This sound is somewhat unique to Korean.

ㅉ						

ㄳ (g yeoksiot, 기격시옷)	ㄳ					
	ㄳ					

넋						
삯						
몫						

ㄵ (rieunjieut, ㄴ은지읒)	ㄵ					
	ㄵ					

앉	다					
얹	다					

| ㄶ
(nieunhieut,
니은히읗) | ㄶ | | | | |
| | ㄶ | | | | |

많	다				
끊	다				
점	잖	다			

| ㄺ
(rieulgiyeok,
리을기역) | ㄺ | | | | |
| | ㄺ | | | | |

흙					
닭					
밝	다				

ㄹㅁ	ㄹㅁ					
(rieulmieum, 리을미음)	ㄹㅁ					

앎						
닮다						
젊다						

ㄹㅂ	ㄹㅂ					
(rieulbieup, 리을비읍)	ㄹㅂ					

넓다						
짧다						
떫다						

| 라人 | 라 | | | | |
| (rieulsiot, 리을시옷) | 라 | | | | |

곬					
외	곬				

| 리E | 리E | | | | |
| (rieultieut, 리을티읕) | 리E | | | | |

핥	다				
훑	다				

ㄹㅍ (rieulpieup, 리을피읖)	ㄹㅍ					
	ㄹㅍ					

읊다						

ㄹㅎ (rieulhieut, 리을히읗)	ㄹㅎ					
	ㄹㅎ					

닳다						
싫다						
옳다						

ㅄ

(bieupsiot,
비읍시옷)

| ㅄ | | | | | |

| ㅄ | | | | | |

| 값 | | | | | | |

| 없 | 다 | | | | | |

| | | | | | | |

Writing Hangeul as a Syllable

The Principles in Writing Hangeul as a Syllable

When the main line of the vowels and the consonants is horizontal, write it from left to right.

When the main line of the vowels and the consonants is vertical, write it from top to bottom.

Hangeul syllables consist of the consonants, the vowels, and sometimes additional consonants, all within a rectangular block.

For the vowels with long horizontal lines including ━ (ㅡ, ㅗ, ㅜ, ㅛ, ㅠ), write the vowel below the preceding consonant. When adding another consonant, write the last consonant below the vowel.

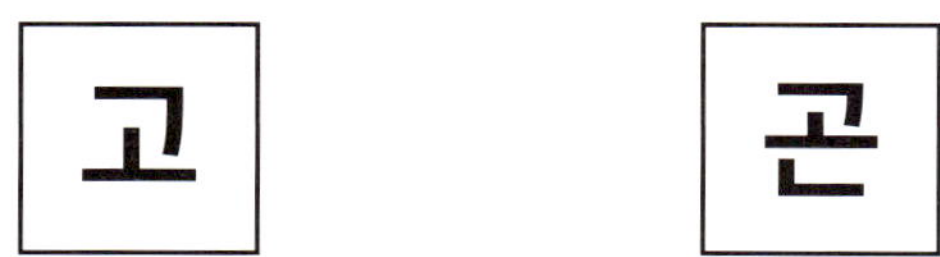

For the vowels with a long vertical line including ㅣ (ㅣ, ㅏ, ㅓ, ㅑ, ㅕ, ㅐ, ㅔ, ㅒ, ㅖ), write the vowel to the right of the preceding consonant. When adding another consonant, write the last consonant below the first consonant-vowel sequence.

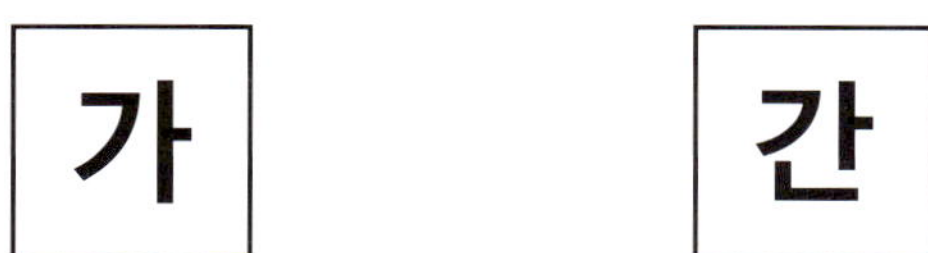

When a vowel includes both — and ㅣ, combine the two forms sequentially from left to right, and then from top to bottom.

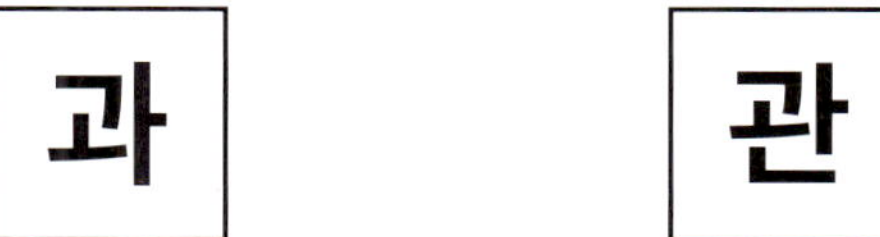

There are 11 special final consonants called double final consonants; ㄳ ㄵ ㄶ ㄺ ㄻ ㄼ ㄽ ㄾ ㄿ ㅀ ㅄ. These letters are only used as final consonants, and are composed of two different basic consonants; ㄱ+ㅅ→ ㄳ . Some letters sound like the first letter of the double final consonants, and some sound like the second letter. For example, 값 sounds like [갑], but 닭 sounds like [닥].

In the case of double consonants, the last consonant should follow at the end of the first consonant; write the two consonants next to each other from left to right under the first consonant-vowel sequence.

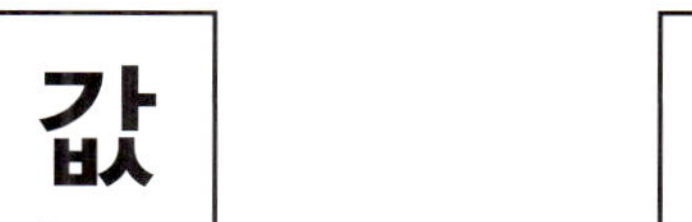

Syllable Writing Practice

	ㅡ	ㅣ	ㅗ	ㅜ	ㅏ	ㅓ	ㅛ	ㅠ	ㅑ	ㅕ
ㄱ	그	기	고	구	가	거	교	규	갸	겨
ㅋ	크	키	코	쿠	카	커	쿄	큐	캬	켜
ㄲ	끄	끼	꼬	꾸	까	꺼	꾜	뀨	꺄	껴
ㄴ	느	니	노	누	나	너	뇨	뉴	냐	녀
ㄷ	드	디	도	두	다	더	됴	듀	댜	뎌
ㅌ	트	티	토	투	타	터	툐	튜	탸	텨
ㄹ	르	리	로	루	라	러	료	류	랴	려
ㄸ	뜨	띠	또	뚜	따	떠	뚀	뜌	땨	뗘
ㅁ	므	미	모	무	마	머	묘	뮤	먀	며
ㅂ	브	비	보	부	바	버	뵤	뷰	뱌	벼
ㅍ	프	피	포	푸	파	퍼	표	퓨	퍄	펴
ㅃ	쁘	삐	뽀	뿌	빠	뻐	뾰	쀼	뺘	뼈
ㅅ	스	시	소	수	사	서	쇼	슈	샤	셔
ㅈ	즈	지	조	주	자	저	죠	쥬	쟈	져
ㅊ	츠	치	초	추	차	처	쵸	츄	챠	쳐
ㅆ	쓰	씨	쏘	쑤	싸	써	쑈	쓔	쌰	쎠
ㅉ	쯔	찌	쪼	쭈	짜	쩌	쬬	쮸	쨔	쪄
ㅇ	으	이	오	우	아	어	요	유	야	여
ㅎ	흐	히	호	후	하	허	효	휴	햐	혀

	ㅡ	ㅣ	ㅗ	ㅜ	ㅏ	ㅓ	ㅛ	ㅠ	ㅑ	ㅕ
ㄱ										
ㅋ										
ㄲ										
ㄴ										
ㄷ										
ㅌ										
ㄹ										
ㄸ										
ㅁ										
ㅂ										
ㅍ										
ㅃ										
ㅅ										
ㅈ										
ㅊ										
ㅆ										
ㅉ										
ㅇ										
ㅎ										

	ㅢ	ㅚ	ㅟ	ㅐ	ㅔ	ㅒ	ㅖ	ㅘ	ㅝ	ㅙ	ㅞ
ㄱ	긔	괴	귀	개	게	걔	계	과	궈	괘	궤
ㅋ	킈	쾨	퀴	캐	케	컈	켸	콰	쿼	쾌	퀘
ㄲ	끠	꾀	뀌	깨	께	꺠	꼐	꽈	꿔	꽤	꿰
ㄴ	늬	뇌	뉘	내	네	냬	녜	놔	눠	놰	눼
ㄷ	듸	되	뒤	대	데	댸	뎨	돠	둬	돼	둬
ㅌ	틔	퇴	튀	태	테	턔	톄	톼	퉈	퇘	퉤
ㄹ	릐	뢰	뤼	래	레	럐	례	롸	뤄	뢔	뤠
ㄸ	띄	뙤	뛰	때	떼	떄	뗴	똬	뚸	뙈	뛔
ㅁ	믜	뫼	뮈	매	메	먜	몌	마	뭐	뫠	뭬
ㅂ	븨	뵈	뷔	배	베	뱨	볘	봐	붜	봬	붸
ㅍ	픠	푀	퓌	패	페	퍠	폐	퐈	풔	퐤	풰
ㅃ	쁴	뾔	쀠	빼	뻬	뺴	쀄	뽜	뿨	뽸	뿀
ㅅ	싀	쇠	쉬	새	세	섀	셰	솨	숴	쇄	쉐
ㅈ	즤	죄	쥐	재	제	쟤	졔	좌	줘	좨	줴
ㅊ	츼	최	취	채	체	챼	쳬	촤	춰	쵀	췌
ㅆ	씌	쐬	쒸	쌔	쎄	썌	쎼	쏴	쒀	쐐	쒜
ㅉ	찍	쬐	쮜	째	쩨	쨰	쪠	쫘	쭤	쫴	쮀
ㅇ	의	외	위	애	에	얘	예	와	워	왜	웨
ㅎ	희	회	휘	해	헤	햬	혜	화	훠	홰	훼

	ㅢ	ㅚ	ㅟ	ㅐ	ㅔ	ㅒ	ㅖ	ㅘ	ㅝ	ㅙ	ㅞ
ㄱ											
ㅋ											
ㄲ											
ㄴ											
ㄷ											
ㅌ											
ㄹ											
ㄸ											
ㅁ											
ㅂ											
ㅍ											
ㅃ											
ㅅ											
ㅈ											
ㅊ											
ㅆ											
ㅉ											
ㅇ											
ㅎ											

	ㅢ	ㅚ	ㅟ	ㅐ	ㅔ	ㅒ	ㅖ	ㅘ	ㅝ	ㅙ	ㅞ
ㄱ	긕	괵	귁	객	겍	걕	곅	곽	궉	괙	궥
ㅋ	킉	쾩	퀵	캑	켁	컉	켹	콱	쿽	쾍	퀙
ㄲ	끡	꾁	뀍	깩	껙	꺡	꼑	꽉	꿕	꽥	꿱
ㄴ	늰	뇐	뉜	낸	넨	냰	녠	놘	눤	놴	뉀
ㄷ	듿	됟	뒫	댇	덷	댿	뎯	돧	둳	됇	뒏
ㅌ	틛	퇻	튇	탣	텓	턛	톋	퇃	퉏	퇟	퉫
ㄹ	릘	뢸	륄	랠	렐	럘	롈	뢀	뤌	뢜	뤨
ㅁ	믬	묌	뮘	맴	멤	먬	묔	뫔	뭠	뫰	뭼
ㅂ	븹	뵙	뷥	뱁	벱	뱹	볩	봡	붭	봽	붹
ㅍ	픱	푑	퓝	팹	펩	퍱	폡	퐙	풥	퐵	풱
ㅅ	싇	쇧	쉳	샏	섿	섇	셷	솯	숻	쇋	쉗
ㅈ	즫	죋	쥗	잳	젣	쟫	졛	좓	줟	좯	줻
ㅊ	츧	쵣	췯	챋	첻	챿	쳳	촫	춷	쵇	췓
ㅆ	씓	쐳	쒿	쌛	쎋	썓	쎳	쏻	쒇	쐗	쒣
ㅇ	읭	욍	윙	앵	엥	얭	옝	왕	웡	왱	웽
ㅎ	힓	횓	휟	핻	헫	햳	혣	홛	훧	홷	휃

	ㅢ	ㅚ	ㅟ	ㅐ	ㅔ	ㅒ	ㅖ	ㅘ	ㅝ	ㅙ	ㅞ
ㄱ											
ㅋ											
ㄲ											
ㄴ											
ㄷ											
ㅌ											
ㄹ											
ㅁ											
ㅂ											
ㅍ											
ㅅ											
ㅈ											
ㅊ											
ㅆ											
ㅇ											
ㅎ											

Writing Practice of Hangeul Words

태극기
Korean flag

한옥
Korean house

태	극	기				
한	옥					
태	극	기				
한	옥					

한복
Korean clothes

무궁화
rose of Sharon

한	복					
무	궁	화				
한	복					
무	궁	화				

불고기

bulgogi

떡볶이

tteokbokki

불	고	기					
떡	볶	이					
불	고	기					
떡	볶	이					

김치

kimchi

치맥

chimaek

김	치					
치	맥					
김	치					
치	맥					

아버지, 아빠		어머니, 엄마	
father		mother	

아	버	지				
아	빠					
어	머	니				
엄	마					

할아버지		할머니	
grandfather		grandmother	

할	아	버	지			
할	머	니				
할	아	버	지			
할	머	니				

딸
daughter

아들
son

딸						
아	들					
딸						
아	들					

누나
older sister (used by males)

언니
older sister (used by females)

누	나					
언	니					
누	나					
언	니					

형		
형 older brother (used by males)		

오빠		
오빠 older brother (used by females)		

형						
오	빠					
형						
오	빠					

남동생		
남동생 younger brother (used by males)		

여동생		
여동생 younger sister (used by females)		

남	동	생				
여	동	생				
남	동	생				
여	동	생				

삼촌	고모
uncle	aunt (father's sister)

삼	촌				
고	모				
삼	촌				
고	모				

이모	조카
aunt (mother's sister)	nephew

이	모				
조	카				
이	모				
조	카				

눈
eye
코
nose
눈
코
눈
코
귀
ear
입
mouth
귀
입
귀
입

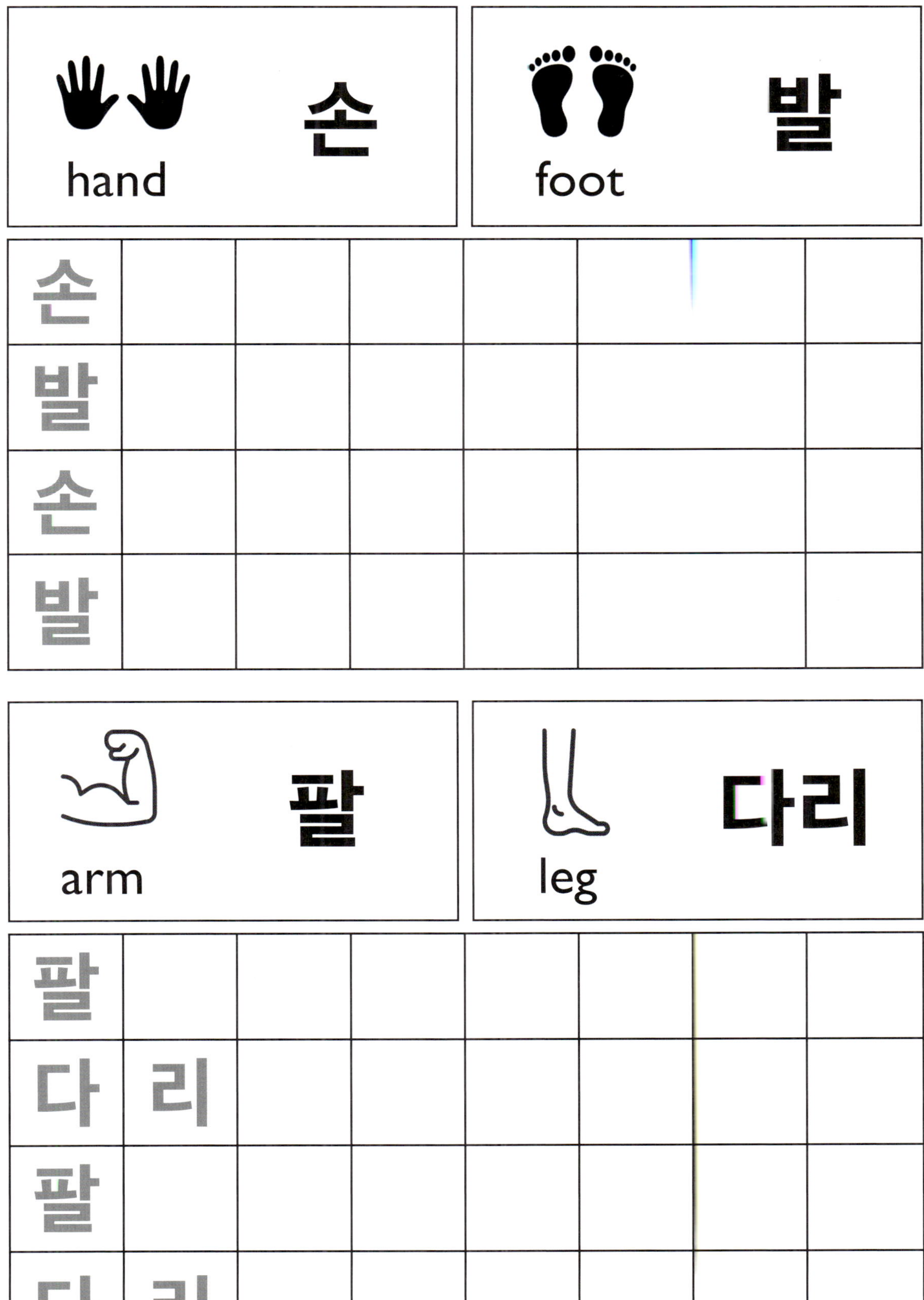

hand
손
foot
발
손
발
손
발
arm
팔
leg
다리
팔
다 리
팔
다 리

봄
spring

여름
summer

봄						
여	름					
봄						
여	름					

가을
fall

겨울
winter

가	을					
겨	울					
가	을					
겨	울					

낮
day

밤
night

낮					
밤					
낮					
밤					

해
sun

달
moon

해					
달					
해					
달					

일, 하나

one

일						
하	나					
하	이					
둘						

이, 둘

two

삼, 셋

three

삼						
셋						
사						
넷						

사, 넷

four

	오, 다섯
five	

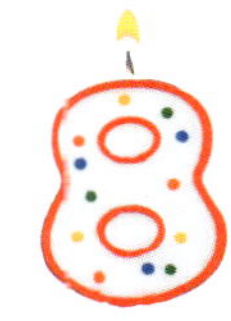

육, 여섯

six

오						
다	섯					
육						
여	섯					

칠, 일곱

seven

팔, 여덟

eight

칠						
일	곱					
팔						
여	덟					

구, 아홉

십, 열

구						
아	홉					
아						
십						
열						

오십

백

오	십					
오	백					
오	십					
오	백					

 **천**

thousand

 **오천**

five thousand

천						
오	천					
천						
오	천					

 **만**

ten thousand

 **오만**

fifty thousand

만						
오	만					
만						
오	만					

 월요일

monday

 화요일

tuesday

월	요	일				
화	요	일				
월	요	일				
화	요	일				

 수요일

wednesday

 목요일

thursday

수	요	일				
목	요	일				
수	요	일				
목	요	일				

금요일

friday

토요일

saturday

금	요	일			
토	요	일			
금	요	일			
토	요	일			

일요일

sunday

공휴일

holiday

일	요	일			
공	휴	일			
일	요	일			
공	휴	일			

pear 배

persimmon 감

배					
감					
배					
감					

tangerine 귤

grape 포도

귤					
포	도				
귤					
포	도				

딸기

strawberry

사과

apple

딸	기				
사	과				
딸	기				
사	과				

참외

Korean melon

수박

watermelon

참	외				
수	박				
참	외				
수	박				

체	리				

체리

cherry

석류

pomegranate

체	리				
석	류				
체	리				
석	류				

키위

kiwi

메론

melon

키	위				
메	론				
키	위				
메	론				

망고

mango

복숭아

peach

망	고				
복	숭	아			
망	고				
복	숭	아			

바나나

banana

무화과

fig

바	나	나			
무	화	과			
바	나	나			
무	화	과			

양파

onion

배추

kimchi cabbage

양	파					
배	추					
양	파					
배	추					

마늘

garlic

파

green onion

마	늘					
파						
마	늘					
파						

호박

pumpkin

감자

potato

호	박				
감	자				
호	박				
감	자				

시금치

spinach

양배추

cabbage

시	금	치			
양	배	추			
시	금	치			
양	배	추			

eggplant

가지

tomato

토마토

가	지				
토	마	토			
가	지				
토	마	토			

bell pepper

피망

mushroom

버섯

피	망				
버	섯				
피	망				
버	섯				

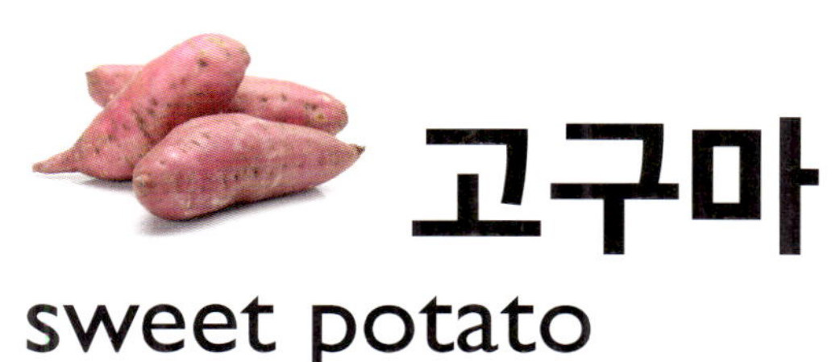

고구마

sweet potato

고추

chili pepper

고	구	마				
고	추					
고	구	마				
고	추					

옥수수

corn

당근

carrot

옥	수	수				
당	근					
옥	수	수				
당	근					

계란

egg

고기

meat

계	란			
고	기			
계	란			
고	기			

닭고기

chicken

소시지

susage

닭	고	기		
소	시	지		
닭	고	기		
소	시	지		

생선

fish

새우

shrimp

생	선					
새	우					
생	선					
새	우					

조개

clam

게

crab

조	개					
게						
조	개					
게						

주전자

kettle

국자

ladle

주	전	자				
국	자					
주	전	자				
국	자					

저울

scale

접시

dish

저	울					
접	시					
저	울					
접	시					

냄비

pot

컵

cup

냄	비				
컵					
냄	비				
컵					

숟가락

spoon

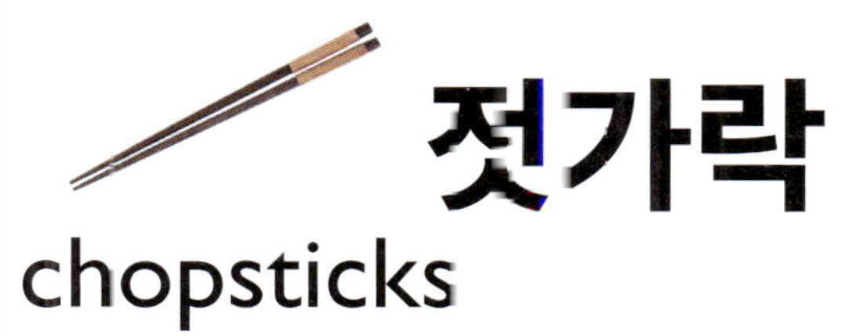

젓가락

chopsticks

숟	가	락		
젓	가	락		
숟	가	락		
젓	가	락		

<table>
<tr><td>
bird</td><td>새</td><td>
pigeon</td><td>비둘기</td></tr>
</table>

새						
비	둘	기				
새						
비	둘	기				

<table>
<tr><td>
duck</td><td>오리</td><td>
turkey</td><td>칠면조</td></tr>
</table>

오	리					
칠	면	조				
오	리					
칠	면	조				

토끼

rabbit

양

sheep

토	끼					
양						
토	끼					
양						

말

horse

개

dog

말						
개						
말						
개						

고양이

cat

호랑이

tiger

고	양	이				
호	랑	이				
고	양	이				
호	랑	이				

개구리

frog

낙타

camel

개	구	리				
낙	타					
개	구	리				
낙	타					

사자

lion

돼지

pig

사	자					
돼	지					
사	자					
돼	지					

코뿔소

rhinocero

얼룩말

zebra

코	뿔	소				
얼	룩	말				
코	뿔	소				
얼	룩	말				

연필

pencil

공책

notebook

연	필				
공	책				
연	필				
공	책				

자

ruler

지우개

eraser

자					
지	우	개			
자					
지	우	개			

책

book

가위

scissors

책					
가	위				
책					
가	위				

볼펜

ball pen

칼

knife

볼	펜				
칼					
볼	펜				
칼					

선풍기
electric fan

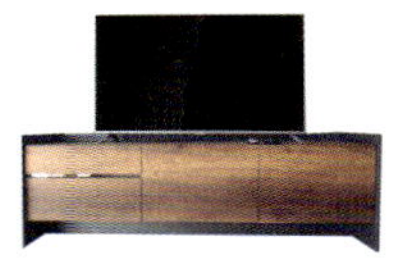
텔레비전
TV

선	풍	기			
텔	레	비	전		
선	풍	기			
텔	레	비	전		

청소기
vacuum

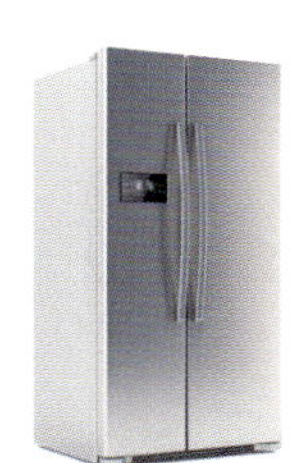
냉장고
refrigerator

청	소	기			
냉	장	고			
청	소	기			
냉	장	고			

책상					
desk					

의자					
chair					

책	상				
의	자				
책	상				
의	자				

침대					
bed					

옷장					
closet					

침	대				
옷	장				
침	대				
옷	장				

<table>
<tr><td>
hat</td><td>모자</td><td>
wallet</td><td>지갑</td></tr>
</table>

모	자				
지	갑				
모	자				
지	갑				

<table>
<tr><td>
shoes</td><td>구두</td><td>
sneakers</td><td>운동화</td></tr>
</table>

구	두				
운	동	화			
구	두				
운	동	화			

가방

handbag

장갑

gloves

가	방					
장	갑					
가	방					
장	갑					

양말

socks

옷

clothes

양	말				
옷					
양	말				
옷					

바지
pants

치마
skirt

바	지					
치	마					
바	지					
치	마					

수영복
swimsuit

안경
glasses

수	영	복				
안	경					
수	영	복				
안	경					

빗

comb

혁대

razor

빗					
혁	대				
빗					
혁	대				

손목
시계

watch

귀걸이

earring

손	목	시	계		
귀	걸	이			
손	목	시	계		
귀	걸	이			

비행기

airplane

버스

bus

비	행	기			
버	스				
비	행	기			
버	스				

자동차

car

자전거

bike

자	동	차			
자	전	거			
자	동	차			
자	전	거			

오토바이
motorcycle

헬리콥터
helicopter

오	토	바	이			
헬	리	콥	터			
오	토	바	이			
헬	리	콥	터			

기차
train

배
ship

기	차					
배						
기	차					
배						

Appendix

Learning Hangeul using the Fingers

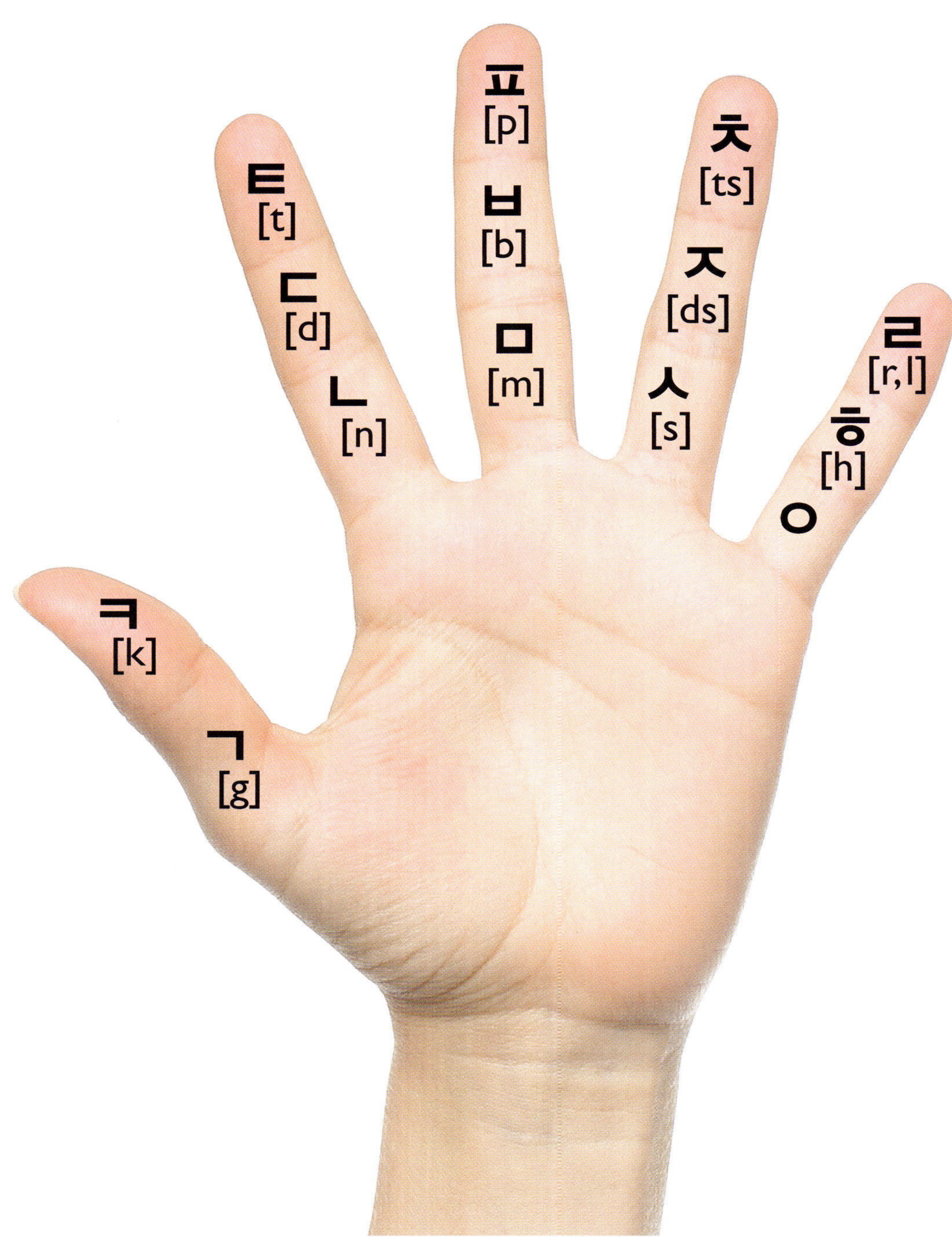

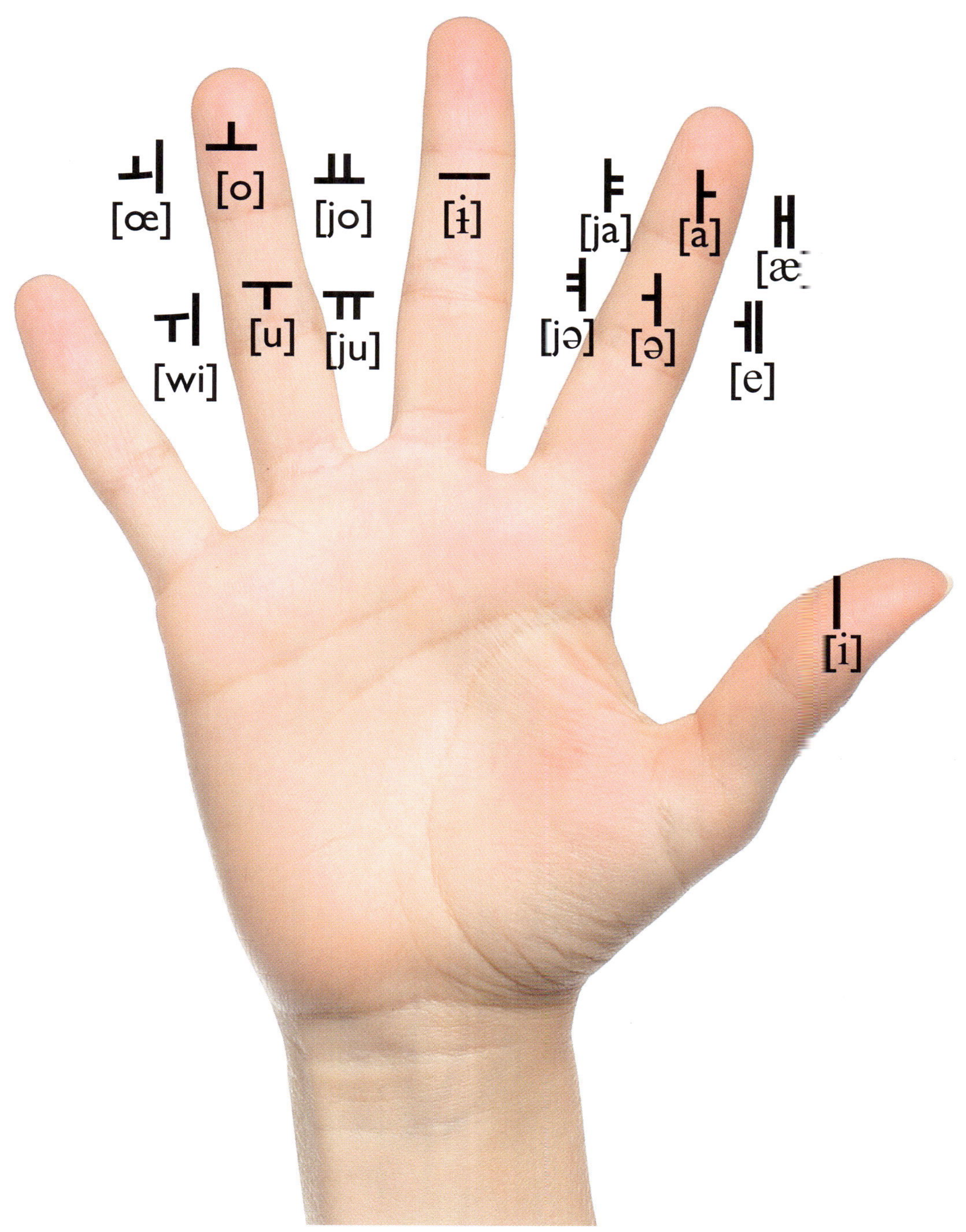

source_ 《Hangeul, the letter for sound of nature》

Places related to Hangeul

국립한글박물관 National Hangeul Museum
https://www.hangeul.go.kr

사진 출처 : 국립한글박물관

한글학회와 주시경 선생 The Korean Language Society and Mr Ju Si-gyeong
https://www.hangeul.or.kr

사진 출처 : 위키피디아

주시경 마당 Ju Si-gyeong Madang

사진 출처 : 내안에 서울

한글 가온길 Hangeul gaongil
http://gaongiltour.com/

1) 한글학회(1구역)

   The Korean Language Society (area 1)

2) 주시경마당(2구역)

   Ju Si-gyeong Madang (area 2)

3) 세종예술의 정원(3구역)

   Sejong Art Garden (area 3)

4) 세종로 공원(4구역)

   Sejong-ro Park (area 4)

5) 세종대왕동상(5구역)

   Statue of King Sejong the Great (area 5)

6) 세종생가터(6구역)

   King Sejong's birthplace (area 6)

사진 출처 : 내안에 서울

한글가온길

이야기를 잇는
한글가온길

사진 출처 : 내 손안에 서울

area 6
세종생가터
King Sejong's birthplace
경복궁역(3호선)
Gyeongbokgung Station (Line 3)
경복궁
Gyeongbokgung
광화문
Gwanghwamun
서울특별시 경찰청
Seoul Metropolitan Police Agency
정부서울청사
Central Government Complex
area 4
대한민국역사박물관
National Museum of Korean History
세종로 공원
Sejong-ro Park
한글글자마당
Hangeul Character Madang
area 5
한글가온길 Hangeul gaongil
주시경집터
Ju Si-gyeong house
area 2
area 3
세종대왕 동상
Statue of King Sejong the Great
주시경마당
Ju Si-gyeong Madang
세종예술의 정원
Sejong Art Garden
Sejong Center
한글가온길 Hangeul gaongil
area 1
한글학회
The Korean Language Society
광화문역
Gwanghwamun Station (Line 5)

세종대왕동상과 세종이야기 The statue of King Sejong the Great and Sejong Story
http://www.sejongstory.or.kr

세종로 공원 Sejong-ro Park
https://parks.seoul.go.kr/parks/detailView

세종예술의 정원 Sejong Art Garden
http://www.sejongpac.or.kr/

여주 세종대왕릉, 영릉 Royal tomb of King Sejong the Great, Yeongneung in Yeoju
https://sejong.cha.go.kr

Let's Learn Korean Alphabet 한글
with King Sejong the Great

First edition publication date | October 9, 2023
Author | Yu Eunsil
Publisher | Yu Eunsil
Publishing Company | Herwonmedia

Address | 19, Pirundae-ro 7-gil, Jongno-gu, Seoul, Republic of Korea
Phone | 82-2-766-9273
Fax | 82-2-766-9272
Website | https://blog.naver.com/herwonmedia
Registration of Publication | No. 300-2005-204 December 2, 2005

© Yu Eunsil

ISBN | 978-89-92162-98-2(93710)
Price | ₩15,000 KOREA $16 USA $20 CAN   €15 EUR